Latin Themes Of Mary Stuart, Queen Of Scots

many times, as seeming to contain real letters, that is to say, historical documents; but, as this was not the case, it was laid aside as useless.

Recently, however, a French scholar, M. Ludovic Lalanne, well known by his historical publications, happening to see this manuscript, examined it more closely, and came to the curious conclusion that it was neither a correspondence, nor a collection or transcripts of real letters, but that it was what French schoolboys call a *cahier de corrigés*, the autograph transcript by Mary Stuart of the Latin, into which she had translated French letters given to her as themes. Under these circumstances the interest of the manuscript was very different from that which it had been supposed to possess, not so great perhaps, but still so curious, that M. Lalanne inserted a description of it, with some well selected extracts naturally taken from the French part, in the weekly Parisian paper, called *l'Atheneum Français,** of which he is the director, and to the

* 1853, 33rd number, Samedi 13th August, pp. 775-7.

who ascertained first the true character of the volume, may be said to have discovered it. I owe to him the knowledge of the book, and I am pleased to have the opportunity of fully expressing all my obligation to his clever article on the subject, without which the present publication would never have seen the light.

The manuscript, written on strong paper, is an 18mo., rather square, measuring 0 095 millimeters in width, by 0.139 in height, and consists of 86 folios, numbered by a later hand.

Its present binding, dating only from the end of the seventeenth century, is plain red morocco; the back is ornamented with *fleurs-de-lys*, and the sides with the arms of France. The edges are gilt, and we will remark that, in gilding the edges, the binder has been careful with them; for it is usual to see the letters closely written at the end of lines to get in an entire word, and the last letters are in no instance cut. It is thus certain that the volume has retained its original shape. On its *garde* is the present number 8660, and, on the

lines: " Maria D. G. Scotor. Reg. Galliæ vero Delphina," thus evidently written after Mary's wedding with Francis, the first son of Henry II, which took place on the 24th of April, 1558, when she was sixteen years of age, and before the accession of her husband to the French throne, which occurred on the 10th of July, 1559; for it was only during that time she could be called *dauphine* of France. Under it is the signature of Ballesdens, which may be seen in the fac-simile, and concerning whom it is here necessary to say a few words, in order to show by whose worthy hands the manuscript was preserved.

Jean Ballesdens was born in Paris at the end of the sixteenth century; he was advocate at the Parliament and Council, and private secretary to the chancellor Pierre Séguier, who was much attached to him, and presented him for election to the Académie Française, of which he was the protector. At a first candidature, Ballesdens, being in competition with the great dramatist, Pierre Corneille, was so just and respectful to the genius

served Ballesdens; for he was the next elected in 1648, in the place of the poet Claude de Malleville, one of the first founders of this literary society. Although Ballesdens held frequent intercourse with all the learned men and authors in his country, he wrote little himself, but, as a true collector of books and manuscripts—for so he was, and many are known signed by him—was rather an editor of the works of others, among which we may quote the *Elogia Clarorum Virorum* by Papyrius Masson; the theological works of *Gregorius Turonensis*; the deeds relating to the acquisition of the Dauphiné by the crown of France; many works by Savonarola; and the Epistles of St. Catharine of Sienna. He died on the 27th of October, 1675.

As already stated, the manuscript contains the French theme and the Latin translation. The Latin, of which the titles are written in capitals with abbreviations reproduced in this edition,* is all by

* It is almost unnecessary to say that the letters S. P. D., frequently used in these directions, are for the words *salutem plurimam dicit.*

written severally and probably day by day. The writing, the pen, the ink, are different, although by the same hand, neat and clever, quite Italian in form, and indisputable, as it will be seen by comparison with the numerous fac-similes of her later handwriting. But it is quite different with the French. It is evident that the book was blank when given to Mary, who was to transcribe her themes on the recto of each leaf, but who sometimes was so inattentive as to write on the verso. When the book was nearly full, the French themes were collected and written in their fit places by one hand, and perhaps at once; for the handwriting is identical in all places, and it is evidently that of a manual copyist; and, as some themes were lost, the leaf waiting them was left blank. This, as well as the character of the letters, though still gothic in their form and very bold, prevents the supposition that the French is a version by her fellow-scholar Elizabeth, from the Latin letters directed to her by Mary; some slight differences furnish also another proof that this French is in fact the original theme, and not a

reader will soon discover some blunders which show evidently the hand of a mere amanuensis.

It would be curious to ascertain the name of this preceptor ; Brantôme does not inform us of it in his article on Mary, but M. Lalanne has judiciously suggested that it is probably indicated in Brantome's article on Elizabeth; she, at least during one year, having had the same preceptor as Mary, as in one of these letters written by him he addresses himself to the two princesses.* The name of her preceptor, therefore, would give the name of the preceptor of Mary. These are the words of Brantôme, speaking of Elizabeth : " Elle avoit beau sçavoir, comme la royne sa mère l'avoit faicte bien estudier par M. de Saint Estienne, un précepteur qu'elle a toujours aimé et respecté jusqu'à sa mort." Some words of the Spanish historian of Mary agree entirely with this hypothesis : " Entregandolo a Catalina de Medicis, reyno de Francia, la fue errando con el mesmo amor que si fuera su madre."† Yet this can only be given as a

* See letter xlv and also letter xxii.
† Antonio di Herrera, Historia de lo Succedido en Esco-

ther facts. And it is very possible that the preceptor of Mary came with her from England, when we bear in mind that this form of letters was used and perhaps traditional in England for the institution of royal pupils; for the very curious book of Latin letters and exercises of Edward VI, when prince, preserved in the Harleian manuscripts, No. 5087 (*Catalogue*, vol. iii, p. 1245), is in all respects a companion to Mary's themes.

As to the turn and form of this education, it was naturally, in accordance with the character of the time, rather profane than sacred. The first letter is an invocation to the sacred muses, and the gods are as frequently cited as God. All the examples are taken from antiquity; Plato, Cicero, and, above all, Plutarch, are the authors most frequently quoted. One modern author appears, however, but one who had so much of an ancient in his spirit, that the rule is confirmed rather than broken by the introduction of Erasmus, of whom are cited

cia e Inglaterra, en quarenta y quatro años que vivio Maria Estuarda, reyna di Escocia. Lisboa, 1590, in 8vo. p. 35 verso.

man Magdalia (*Abbatis et eruditæ*), of which there was then a well known and elegant translation in French verses by the amiable poet Clement Marot, and published about this time; and the dialogue of Philodoxus with Simbulus (letter xxxiv); and it is to be inferred from these quotations that the whole book of the *Colloquia* was read by the royal girls.

Generally the letters are on separate subjects, but in one instance they form a series. It had been said by one of the court, probably before the royal girls, and by allusion, perhaps, to the turn of their education, that women had nothing to do with learning; and, by way of justification for himself and encouragement to his pupils, the preceptor fills fifteen letters (xxvi—xl) with the names of learned girls and women. His learning was easy; numerous were the books on illustrious women, and perhaps he did not even seek so far. In one place (letter xxxv) he speaks of a certain Cassandra Fidelis as praised by Politianus in some one of his Epistles, and when we refer to

women, and with the commentary of Franciscus Silvius in the Parisian edition of 1523, in 4to., it contains almost all the names used by the preceptor.

But with these subjects, which are little more than commonplaces, these themes would have no more to recommend them to curiosity than the themes of the duke of Burgundy,—with this difference still, that M. de St. Etienne or Mary's preceptor, whoever he was, is not a stylist like Fénélon. Happily, and this does honour to the understanding of the former, he has given interest to his themes, and that for us as well as for his pupils, in making them real letters to living and neighbouring persons; they have thus in them something of the life of the times.

The letters are in number LXIV; two only, XLI and XLIV, are directed by the preceptor to Mary; but the ordinary correspondent of Mary is her fellow-student Elizabeth, daughter to King Henry II, who was to be married to the melancholy Spanish king, Philip the Second, and in 1554 was

other daughter of the French king, but younger, being born in November 1547, who married in 1559 the duke of Lorraine, Charles the Third, and to whom certainly relates the childish allusion in letter XXII.

By the direction of the tenth letter we learn the name of another fellow-student of Mary, whose presence is even more curious, from the circumstance that this other fellow-student is not a girl but a boy. Unhappily the Latin form involves the name in a doubt, only to be removed by chance. I confess I cannot guess what may be in French the name *Quarlocoius ;* is it not possible that he was, perhaps, the son of some great Scotch nobleman, who came into France with his young queen? I leave the question, however, to the learning of the Scottish antiquaries.

The other correspondents of Mary were her uncle the famous duke of Guise (letters XXIII, XXIV), and the French dauphin, who was soon to be her husband. One, the XVIIIth, is directed to a man whose name it is singular to see in this place,

edition of his book *l'Institution Chrétienne* was published by Robert Etienne in 1553: as is well known, one part of it is occupied with the negation of purgatory, and the letter is precisely on this point. Was the letter ever sent? It is rather improbable. The others—I speak not of those to Elizabeth, which were to be versions to her—being directed to friends and relatives, who were curious and proud to see the progress of Mary's learning, were certainly sent. But the letter to Calvin stands in a different light. The fact of a letter to him from such a princess—her youth also would have shown it was dictated to her and consequently avowed—would have been too important to be easily admitted. It is, I think, necessary to reduce the question to lesser proportions, and suppose that, the book of Calvin and his opinion on purgatory having been spoken of before the young queen, the preceptor thought good to introduce them in his next lesson to his pupil. However, and whatever may be the case, it is curious to see this childish letter to Calvin, and to think how

ciple, John Knox.

Some names of places are written at the end of some letters, generally in the French part, and interesting, because we see by them the town or castle where the court was, and Mary with it. The names which occur under these circumstances are those of Rheims, I—IV; Compiegne, V—VIII, XI—XIII, XV, XVII, XVIII, XX; Villers Cotterets, XXV—VI; Paris, XXXVI, XXXVIII; Saint Germain, XLI, XLII, XLVI—VIII, LIII, LVI—LX.

For the dates, however scarce, they are not only curious but important, since they tell us the age of the young Mary when she was put to this discipline and occupied with these exercises. From them it may be ascertained that this occupation existed between the 26th July and the 9th January following (letters V and LXI), that is to say, during seven months of the life of Mary, of which these faded pages are the only memorial. For the year, nothing would have indicated it, if it were not positively written in four letters; for we find these dates, " 25 *d'aoust* 1554," " 12 *d'oc-*

XXXVI, LVII, LVIII. A remark is here necessary. The date of the 5th January 1554, which would be 1555 according to the new style, is, as it was to be expected, written according to the old style, in which the year began on the 25th of March.

But Mary, although continuing to write 1554 after a letter dated 26th December and another dated the day of St. John the Evangelist after Christmas, that is to say, the 27th December,— writes in the letters immediately following : *the last day of this year* 1554, using thus at the same time the two manners of ending the year. It is only a new proof, that if the ordonnance which in France made the year begin with January was rendered only by Charles the Ninth, in 1563, the use, thus made official and legal, was in fact already established. An observation curious to make, before leaving this date of 1554, is, that the same year is inscribed by Mary in her prayer-book, preserved at St. Petersburg, and described by Prince Labanoff in the last volume of his edition of the letters of Mary. On one leaf of it may be read, in her

Marie, Royne. 1554."

One word more, and I will close this already too long an introduction. Much has been said on the early learning of Mary. The great credit she has received on this account will be perhaps a little destroyed by this publication; for the reader will see her knowledge of the Latin to be not very sound nor firm, and some blunders are of such a nature as to render us somewhat incredulous as to her own knowledge at this period of life. The admiration, inspired by the praise bestowed by Brantôme on the famous Latin speech delivered in the French court, will be somewhat impaired by the thought that it was a little after our themes, which perhaps were given to her as a first preparation towards this subject, and show us that she was certainly not unaided in the composition of her speech. However, the words of Brantôme, in his life of Mary, are worthy of being quoted here, because they relate to the same period and the same nature of ideas :

" Pour la beauté de l'ame, elle estoit toute pareille; car elle s'estoit faicte fort sçavante en

c

... ., ..., ..

toute la cour, publiquement en la salle du Louvre,
une oraison en latin qu'elle avoit faicte, soubtenant
et deffendant, contre l'opinion commune, qu'il
estoit bien séant aux femmes de sçavoir les lettres
et arts libéraux. Songez quelle rare chose c'estoit
et admirable de voir ceste sçavante et belle reine
ainsy orer en latin, qu'elle entendoit et parloit
fort bien ; car je l'ay veue là : et fut heureux de
faire faire à Antoine Fochain de Chauny en Ver-
mandois, et l'adresser à ladicte reine, une rhétorique en françois, afin qu'elle l'entendist mieux,
et se fist plus éloquente en françois, comme elle
l'a esté, et mieux que si dans la France mesme
elle avoit pris naissance."

This indication of a French treatise on rhetoric
made for Mary was too curious to be overlooked,
because some new facts were to be hoped in it;
and we were not deceived in our expectations,
since the book gives a more precise date to the de-
livering of the speech. For the dedication of the
book* to Mary by Antoine Fouquelin, of Chauny

* Paris, André Wechel, 1555 and 1557, in 8vo.

of the speech was made at the beginning of 1555, immediately perhaps after the cessation of the themes, which were probably given to her as a preparation to it, and this is rendered nearly certain by the circumstance, that most of these letters are on the same subject as the speech, that is on the conveniency of learning for the female sex. The words of Fouquelin are less known but more curious than those of Brantôme, and they therefore deserve to be quoted :

" En quoy, Madame, tout ce que j'en puis avouer mien, vous avez esté la première à qui je l'ay estimé devoir estre voué et dédié, comme à une princesse née, et, selon la commune opinion, divinement prédestinée, non seulement pour l'amplification et avancement de notre langue, mais aussi pour l'illustration et honneur de toute science. De quoy vous me semblâtes donner un certain présage, alors qu'en la présence du Roy, accompaigné de la pluspart des seigneurs de la cour, vous soutenés par une oraison bien latine, et défendiés contre la commune opinion, qu'il estoit

libéraux. Au quel endroit je diroys en quelle admiration d'un chacun vous auriés esté ouye, et
quelle espérance auroit esté conçue de vous par
toute cette noble compaignie, si je le pouvois dire
sans soubçon de flatterie. Ce que j'aime mieux
estre tellement quellement exprimé par ce vers
d'Ovide, parlant de Germanicus Cæsar, petit fils
d'Auguste, élég. 5 du 2 de Pont.

> " ' Quant ta bouche céleste eut ouvert ton soucy,
>   L'on eut dit que les dieux souloient parler ainsi,
>   Et que d'un prince estoit digne telle excellence,
>   Tant avoit de douceur ta divine éloquence.'

Que pleut à votre Majesté que j'eusse pu finer de
cette tant élégante oraison, ou plutôt de la Fran-
çoyse traduction qu'il vous en pleut faire quelque
tems après ; il ne m'eust esté besoin chercher si
loing des exemples, etc."

By this it will be seen that this speech was then
preserved in two forms, in Latin and in French,
and I suppose the last to have been less a translation by Mary, than the original given to her
by her preceptor to be by her put in Latin.
Perhaps it exists, and owes to its commonplace

to this day. With the indication of Fouquelin it will be now easily recognised when met with; but, as its discovery may be only accidental, I am satisfied to leave the honour of it to more fortunate inquirers.

Paris, 31st May, 1855.

1. Legebam heri apud Æsopum fabulam
2. ~~papere~~ pauperem populum est leo rugi-
3. mihi lego ab hinc duobus diebus ~~de~~ dialogu
4. Carneades dicebat, spectatissime auuncu
5. idem petiit iterum suos dies · Quinq̃z
6. institutum · Vale · izj · Septembris ·
7. Sæpe scripsit Marcellæ Romanę propter
8. ficis Pij · 2 · meruit immortale
9. apud S̄L Germanum + die ultimo anni 1554
10. crter egnum qui non sit preditus aliqua virtute ·

De Compiegne 25 · d'Aoust · 1554 ·
d'acquidair de la Dortrin . A S⁺ Germain
dermier jour de nr̃m an 1554 ·

Balliefden

THE FACSIMILE

Represents, first, the title of the theme addressed to Claudius Quarlocojus, p. 13 of the present edition, with ten examples of Mary's handwriting taken from different themes, namely :—

1.	From theme	vi,	page	7.
2.	„	xvi,	„	21.
3.	„	xix,	„	23.
4.	„	xxiii,	„	29.
5.	„	xxiv,	„	31.
6.	„	xxix,	„	39.
7.	„	xxxviii,	„	49.
8.	„	xxxix,	„	51.
9.	„	lvii,	„	71.
10.	„	lxii,	„	77.

Two dates from the French text, being the conclusions of

Theme xxii, page 28, and
„   lvii,   „   70.

And, lastly, the signature of J. Ballesdens.

SCRIBEBAM heri, dilectissima soror, quod virtus venit de studio bonarum literarum. Quare eædem sunt magis necessariæ nobis principibus quàm privatis. Nam ut princeps subditis suis vult antecellere divitijs, potestate, autoritate, et imperio: sic debet inter omnes excellere prudentia, consilio, bonitate, gratia, et omni genere virtutis. Qua de re hierogliphica Ægyptiorum notaverunt oculum in sceptro regum, dicebant enim nullam virtutem magis principem decere quàm prudentiam.

IV.

M. R. SCOTORUM ELIZABETÆ SORORI S. P. D.

QUUM igitur princeps debet antecellere privatis non voluptatibus delicijsve, sed sensu, temperantia, et prudentia: et suum officium anteponere utilitatis reip. suis: opus est (soror omnium charissima) nos dare operam ut sapiamus, exemplo Appellis pictoris, qui tanta fuit in arte sua diligentia ut nullus præteriret dies in quo non ipse lineam aliquam penicillo duxisset. Vale, et me ama ut soles.

JE ne me puis assez ebahi de quoi sur les fautes d'autrui nous sommes plus clairs voians qu'Argus, qui avoit cent yeus. Mais pour voir et corriger les notres, nous sommes plus aveugles que la taupe. C'est de quoi se mocque Æsope, qui dit qu'en la besace de devant nous portons les vices d'autrui, et en celle qui pend derriere nous mettons les notres. Ne faisons ainsi, ma seur, car celui qui veut parler d'autrui doit estre sans culpe. De Compienne ce 26. Juillet.

VI.

HIER je lisoi une fable en Æsope autant profitable que plaisante. La formis en temps d'hyver faisoit bonne chere du blé qu'elle avoit amassé en esté, quand la cicade aiant grand fain vint à elle, pour lui demander à manger. Mais la formis lui dit, Que faisois-tu en esté ? Je chantoi, dit-elle. Si tu chantois en esté, repondit la formis, saulte maintenant en hyver. La fable signifie, ma seur, que pendant que sommes jeunes devons mettre peine d'apprendre des lettres et vertus

Non possum satis mirari quod simus oculatiores in
errores alienos quam Argus, qui habebat centum
oculos : sed ut videamus et emendemus nostros, sumus
cæciores talpa. Qua de re Æsopus ridebat, et dicebat
nos ferre aliena vitia in mantica quæ dependet ad
pectus, et in alia quæ ad tergum ponimus nostra.
Ne ita faciamus, soror dilectissima, nam qui de alijs
vult loqui, debet esse sine culpa. Vale.

VI.

MA. SCOTORUM REGINA ELIZABETÆ SORORI S. P. D.

Legebam heri apud Æsopum fabulam non minus
utilem quam urbanam. Formica hyeme laute vivebat
tritico quod collegerat æstate, quando cicada laborans
fame venit ad illam, et petebat cibum. Sed formica
dicit, Quid faciebas æstate ? Cantabam, dixt. *(sic)*.
Si tu canebas æstate, hyeme salta. Fabula significat
(suavissima soror) nos debere (dum iuvenes sumus)
dare.   .   .   .   .

VII.

J'AI entendu par notre maitre, ma seur ma mignonne, que maintenant vous estudiés fort bien, de quoi je suis très joieuse, et vous prie de continuer, comme pour le plus grand bien que sauriés avoir en ce monde. Car ce que nous a donné nature est de peu de durée, et le redemandera en viellesse, ou plus tost. Ce que nous a presté fortune elle nous l'ostera aussi. Mais ce que vertu (laquelle procede des bonnes lettres) nous donne, est immortel, et le garderons a jamais. A Compienne. 25. Juillet.

VIII.

CATON disoit, ma seur, que l'entendement d'un chacun est semblable au fer, lequel tant plus est manié, de tant plus reluyt. Mais quand on le laisse en repos il devient rouillé. Ce que tesmoigne bien Cicero au livre des

M. SC. R. EL. SORORI S. P. D.

Audivi a nostro præceptore, soror integerrima, te
studere optime, ex quo gaudeo, et te deprecor ut sic
pergas, nam est excellentissimum bonum quod posis *(sic)*
habere.   Quod enim natura dedit, parum durat, et
repetet in senectute vel prius.   Quod mutuo dedit
fortuna deponet etiam.   Sed quod virtus, quæ pro-
cedit a bonarum literarum lectione, donat, est immortale et nostrum semper erit.   Vale.

VIII.

M. SC. R. ELIZABETÆ SUAVISSIMÆ SORORI S. P. D.

Cato ingenium uniuscuiusque dicebat, soror, ferro
esse simile, quod usu splendescit, at in otio rubigine
obducitur: id quod Cicero testatur in libro de claris
oratoribus, quando dicit se singulis diebus scribere

Latin. Et d'avantage, croiés, ma seur, qu'oisiveté est la mère de tous vices. Par quoi il nous faut a toutes heures exercer notre esprit en erudition ou en vertu. Car l'exercer en choses vainnes et mechantes, ce n'est l'exercer mais le corrompre. A Compiene 28. Juillet.

IX.

Ce n'est pas sans cause, mes seurs très aimées, que la roine nous commandoit hier de faire ce que nous diront noz gouvernantes. Car Cicero dit, tout au commancement du second livre des Lois, que celui qui scait bien commander a autresfois obei. Et que quicunque modestement obeit est digne de commander une fois. Plutarque, auteur digne de foi, a dit que les vertus s'apprennent par preceptes aussi bien que les arts. Et use de cet argument. Les hommes apprennent a chanter, a sauter, les lettres aussi, a laborer la terre, a se tenir a cheval, a se chausser, a se vestir, a faire cuisine. Et penserons-nous que vaincre ses affections, commander en une Rep. (chose entre toutes très difficile), bien conduire une armée, mener bonne vic, penserons-

Quapropter opus est omnibus horis exercere ingenium
nostrum eruditione vel virtute, nam exercere rebus
vanis aut flagitiosis hoc non exercere est sed corrum-
pere. Vale. 5. Cal. Augusti.

IX.

M. SC. R. ELIZABETÆ ET CLAUDIÆ SORORIBUS S. D. P.

Non abs re (suavissimæ sorores) regina jubebat heri
nobis facere id quod gubernatrices dicent. Nam Cicero
sic ait in principio secundi libri de legibus. Ille qui
bene scit imperare, aliquando obedivit, et qui modeste
obedit est dignus imperare aliquando. Plutarchus autor
locuples ait virtutes discendas esse præceptis ut aliæ
artes, et utitur illo argumento. Homines discunt can-
tare, saltare, literas, colere terram, equo insidere,
calceari, vestiri, et coquere: et nos credemus vincere
vluptates *(sic)*, imperare reipublicæ (quæ res inter
omnes difficilima est) ducere exercitum, instituere
vitam, credemus, inquam, id evenire fortuito? Ne
hoc credamus, sed discamus, obediamus hoc tempore,

age.   29 Juillet.

X.

POUR quelques vertus, scavoir, ou autres graces que tu
aies, ne t'en glorifie point, mais plus tost donnes en
louange a Dieu qui seul est cause de ce bien.   Ne te
mocque de personne, mais pense que ce qui advient a
un, il peut advenir a chacun.   Et, comme ja je t'ai dit,
ren graces a Dieu de quoi il t'a mis hors de tel povre
sort, et prie que telle chose ne t'avienne, et aide a
l'affligé si tu puis.   Car si tu es misericordieus aus
hommes, tu obtiendras misericorde de Dieu.   Au quel
je prie vouloir favoriser a toutes tes entreprinses.
1 jour d'Aoust.

XI.

LE meilleur heritage qui peut estre delaissé aux enfans
des bons parens, c'est la voie de vertu, et la connoissance

ætatem. Bene valete. 3. Cal, Augusti.

X.

MA. SC. REGINA CLAUDIO QUARLOCOIO CONDISCIPULO S. P. D.

QUIBUSCUNQUE virtutibus, sapientia, eruditione, et aliis
gratiis præditus sis, ne gloriare, sed potius da gloriam
Deo qui solus caussa est tanti boni. Neminem irrideto irrideto *(sic)*, sed puta quod evenit uni posse
accidere omnibus. Et, ut jam dixi tibi, age gratias
Deo omnipotenti quod te posuerit extra sortem tam
miseram et precare ut talis res non tibi eveniat. Sub-
veni afflicto si possis, nam si tu fueris misericors aliis,
consequeris misericordiam adeo (*sic, pro* a Deo), quem
deprecor ut faveat omnibus tuis cœptis. Vale.

XI.

M. SC. R. ELIZABETÆ ET CLAUDIÆ SORORIBUS S. P. D.

OPTIMA hereditas quæ potest relinqui liberis a bonis
parentibus est via virtutis, cognitio plurium artium,

riche patrimoine. Par quoi je ne sauroi assés louer la prudence du roy et de la royne, qu'ils veullent que notre jeune age soit imbut et de bonnes meurs et de lettres, suivant l'opinion de plusieurs sages, qui n'ont tant estimé bien n'aistre, (*sic*, *for* naistre), que bien estre institué. Dont, mes seurs, de notre costé, faisons nostre devoir. A Compienne. 7. jour d'Aoust.

XII.

Pour ce que la vraie amitié, de la quelle je vous aime plus que moi-mesme, me commande que tout le bien qu'aurai jamais sera commun entre nous, ma seur, je vous vueil bien faire participante d'une belle similitude que je leu hier en Plutarque. Tout ainsi, dit-il, que qui empoisonne une fontaine publique, de laquelle chacun boit, n'est digne d'un seul supplice : ainsi est très malheureus et mechant qui gaste l'esprit d'un prince, et qui ne lui corrige ses mauvaises opinions, qui redonderont a la perte de tant de peuple. Par quoi, ma seur, il nous faut ouir et obeir a ceux qui nous remontrent. De Compienne. 8. d'Aoust.

satis laudare prudentiam regis reginæque nostræ, qui
volunt hanc nostram rudem ætatem imbui bonis mori-
bus et literis : sequuti opinionem plurimorum homi-
num sapientum, qui præclarius duxerunt bene institui
quam bene nasci.   Quare quantum ad nos attinet,
fungamur nostro officio.   Valete.

XII.

M. SC. R. EL. SORORI S. D. P.

QUUM vera amicitia qua te ante me amo, soror, imperet
mihi ut omne bonum quod unquam habebo sit inter
nos commune, volo te facere participem pulcherrimæ
similitudinis quam heri legebam apud Plutarchum.
Nam, inquit ille, quemadmodum qui inficit veneno
fontem publicum, de quo omnes bibunt, non est dignus
solo supplicio, ita ille est infelicissimus et nocentissimus
qui inficit animum principis et qui non emendat malas
opiniones quæ redundent in perniciem multorum.
Quare, soror, oportet nos obedire iis qui nos corripiunt.

XIII.

C'est pour vous inciter a lire Plutarque, ma mie, et ma bonne seur, que si souvent en mes epitres je fai mension de lui. Car c'est un philosophe digne de la leçon d'un prince. Mais oiés qu'il adioute au propos que je vous tenoi hier. Si, dit-il, celui qui gaste et contrefait la monnoie du prince est puni, combien est plus digne de supplice qui corrout l'entendement d'icelui? Car, ma seur, quels sont les princes en la Rep., disoit Platon, tels ont accoutumé d'estre les citoiains. Et pensoit les Rep. estre bien heureuses, qui etoient gouvernées par princes, et doctes, et sages. De Compienne, 9. d'Aoust.

XIV.

La vraie grandeur et excellence du prince, ma très aimée seur, n'est en dignité, en or, en pourpre, en pierreries, et autres pompes de fortune : mais en prudence, en vertu, en sapience, et en scavoir. Et d'autant que le prince veut estre different a son peuple d'habit, et de façon de vivre, d'autant doit-il estre eloigné des folles opinions du vulgaire. Adieu, et m'aimés autant que vous pourrés. 10 d'Aoust.

XIII.

M. R. S. EL. SORORI S. P. D.

QUUM tam sæpe facio mentionem Plutarchi, amica summa mea et soror, in meis epistolis, hoc facio ut ad hunc legendum te incitem. Nam est philosophus dignus lectione principis. Sed audi quomodo perficit propositum quod heri scribebam ad te: Si is qui viciat monetam principis punitur, quantopere ille est dignior supplicio qui corrumpit ingenium ejus. Profecto quales sunt principes in Rep. dicebat Plato, tales solent esse cives, et Resp. felicissimas putabat si à doctis et sapientibus principibus regerentur. Vale.

XIV.

M. SC. R. EL. SORORI S. P. D.

VERA principis majestas non est in amplitudine, in dignitate, auro, purpura, gemmis et aliis pompis fortunæ: sed in prudentia, sapientia et eruditione. Verum quantopere princeps vult abesse ab habitu et victu plebeio, tantopere ille debet etiam abesse à sordidis opinionibus et stul[ti]tiis vulgi. Vale et me ama quantum poteris.

C

Pour toujours, selon ma coutume, vous faire participante de mes bonnes leçons, je vous vueil bien dire comme j'apprenoi devant hier que le prince ne doit vanter les armes, et autres enseignes de noblesse qu'il a de ses parens : mais plus tost doit suivre et exprimer les vertus et bonnes meurs d'iceulx. Car, ma seur, la vraie noblesse c'est vertu. Et le second poinct que doit avoir le prince, c'est qui soit instruict de la connoissance des arts et sciences. Le tiers, et qui est le moindre, qui soit orne des paintures et armes de ses predecesseurs. Et de cettui nous sommes asses ornées. Efforceons-nous donc d'avoir le premier. Adieu. De Compienne. 13. d'Aoust.

Je lisoi anjourdhui, ma seur, que Platon appelloit les princes gardes de la Rep. Et dit qu'il faut qu'ils soient a leurs païs ce que les chiens sont au troppeau. Et appelle le prince cruel et tyrant, lion. Sainct Paul parlant de Neron l'appelloit ainsi. Je suis, disoit-il, delivré de la bouche du lion. Le sage Salomon a

Le prince mauvais sur son povre peuple est un lion rugissant et un ours affamé. Apprenons donc maintenant les vertus, ma seur, lesquelles nous rendront chiens fideles a nos troppeaus, et non loups, ni ours, ni lions. Mon maitre m'a dit que vous trouvés mal, je vous irai tantost voir. Ce pendant je vous di adieu. 14. d'Aoust.

XVII.

Si en notre jeune age nous apprenons les vertus, ma seur, ainsi que je vous ecrivoi hier, le peuple ne nous appellera jamais loups ni ours, ni lions, mais nous honorera, et aimera comme les enfans ont coutume aimer les peres et meres. Le propre d'un bon prince est ne blecer personne, profiter a tous, mesmement aux siens. Et que cette vois tyrannique soit loin de son entendement. Je le vueil ainsi, je le commande ainsi, et pour toute raison ma volonté soit. Car, ma seur, cette vois est vraie qui ja est allée en proverbe, ils haient quand ils craignent. A Dieu. Ce 17. d'Aoust. A Compienne.

depinxit tyrannum principem. Impius princeps, inquit, super pauperem populum est leo rugiens et ursus esuriens. Nunc igitur discamus, soror, virtutes omnes, quæ nos efficient canes fideles nostris gregibus, non lupos, non ursos, neque leones. Præceptor meus dixit mihi te laborare ventre, ego statim te visam. Cura interim ut bene valeas.

XVII.

M. SC. R. EL. SORORI S. P. D.

Si in hac nostra juventa ætate didiscerimus virtutem, ut heri dicebam, nunquam populus nos appellabit lupos, ursos, neque leones, sed nos amabit et colet ut pueri solent amare parentes. Proprium boni principis est ledere neminem, omnibus præsertim suis. Denique vox illa tyrannica absit ab animo principis,

Sic volo, sic iubeo, sit pro ratione voluntas.

Est enim ista vox vera quæ iam abijt in proverbium, Oderint dum metuunt. Bene vale, suauissima soror.

Socrates disoit qu'il i avoit deus voies par lesquelles les espris sortent du corps. Car ceus qui se sont gardés chastes et entiers, et qui aus corps humains ont ensuivi la vie des Dieus, ils retornent facilement a eus. Et ceus qui se sont du tout souillés de vices, ont un chemin detorné du conseil, et de la presence des Dieus. Mais les espris de ceus qui se sont quasi fais serviteurs des voluptés, et non toutesfois du tout, sont long temps a errer par la terre avant que de retorner au ciel. Tu vois donc que Socrates, Platon, et plusieurs autres philosophes ethniques, ont eu cognoissance du purgatoire que toi, doué de la loi de grace, miserablement et a ta perte tu nies. Jesuchrist le fils de Dieu te vueille rapeller, Calvin. De Compienne. 18. d'Aoust.

XIX.

Vous ebahisses, ma seur, pour quoi je sorti hier de la chambre de la Royne, veu qu'il estoit dimenche, pour aller en mon estude. Croies que depuis deux jours je li un colloque d'Erasme qu'il appelle Diluculum, tant beau, tant joieus, et tant utile que rien plus. He

est la plus precieuse. Davantage le latin i est si facile, et si elegant, qui n'est possible d'estre plus poli. Je le vous expliquerai aujourdhui si j'ai loisir. Adieu. Ce 20. d'Aoust.

XX.

PLUTARQUE dit que la colere et la mauvaitié est plus dangereuse en un prince qu'en une personne privee : d'autant que le prince a puissance de beaucoup offencer et l'autre non. Et pour ce a bon droict requiert il doctrine et prudence en un prince. Car comme disoit Bias, l'un des sept sages de Grece, l'œuvre du sage est (combien qui soit offencé) de ne nuire a personne, encores qu'il en ait la puissance. En quoi il ensuit la bonte de Dieu, lequel ne fait rien si souvent ni si volontiers que de pardonner. A Compienne, 23. d'Aoust.

re præciosissima præciosissimum est. Præterea sermo
latinus adeo purus, et elegans est, ut politior esse non
possit. Explicabo tibi hodie si licuerit per otium.
Vale. 20. Aug.

M. SC. R. EL. SORORI S. P. D.

PLUTARCUS dicit iram et malitiam esse in principe
periculosiorem, quam in priuatis. Nam princeps potest plurimum offendere, alter vero minime. Quapropter requirit doctrinam et prudentiam in principe.
Nam quomodo dicebat Bias, unus septem sapientum
Græciæ, opus sapientis est (quamuis offensus sit) nocere
nemini etiam si possit. Qua in re sequitur bonitatem
Dei qui nihil sæpius facit, nec libentius quam parcere.
Bene vale.

XXI.

JE croi, ma seur, le dict de Magdalia, que lisions hier
en Erasme, estre très veritable, a scavoir, nul ne
pouvoit vivre suavement, si ne vit bien.   Aussi
mettoit Bias le souverain bien en la vertu de l'esprit,
et la plus g[r]ande misere en vice et en la malice des
hommes. Car, comme dit Cicero au livre de viellesse, la
souvenance de plusieurs beaus actes est très plaisante ;
et au contraire, comme tesmoigne le sage en ses pro-
verbes, crainte est touiours avec ceus qui font mal.
Et Plaute dit que rien n'est si miserable que l'esprit
qui se sent coulpable de quelque mal faict.   Pour ce,
ma seur, sur toute chose estudions a Vertu. 24. d'Aoust.

XXII.

QUAND hier au soir mon maitre vous prioit de reprendre votre seur, de quoi elle vouloit boire se
voulant mettre au lict : vous lui repondistes que vous
mesme voulies boire aussi. Voiés donc, ma seur,
quelles nous devons estre qui sommes l'exemple du
peuple.   Et comme oserons-nous reprendre les autres,
si nous mesme ne sommes sans faute ?   Il faut qu'un

CREDO ego, soror suavissima, sententiam Magdaliæ quam legebamus heri apud Erasmum esse verissimam, neminem posse viuere suauiter nisi bene viuat. Quare Bias ponebat summum bonum in solo animi virtute æt maiorem et miseriam (*sic*) in vitiis et malitia hominis. Nam, ut Cicero ait in libro de senectute, multorum acto- rum recordatio jucundissima est, contra, ut sapiens tes- tatur in prouerbiis, Pauor est iis qui operantur malum. Et Plautus dicit nihil esse miserius quam animus sibi conscius. Quæ cum ita sint, soror, studeamus virtuti. Vale.

XXII.

M. SC. R. EL. SORORI S. P. D.

QUUM heri sero meus præceptor te deprecabatur ut reprehenderes sororem tuam quod vellet bibere volens discedere cubitum, respondisti te non audere, quia ipsa volebas potare. Vide ergo, soror, quales nos debemus esse quæ sumus exemplum populo quomodo igitur audebimus alios emendare nisi sine errore fuerimus. Oportet bonum principem vivere ad hunc

qu'en sa maison il ne puisse estre reprins de personne. Et que dehors ne soit veu que faisant, ou pensant chose pour l'utilité publique. Et doit avoir grand cure que sa parole ne sente rien que vertu. Soions donc du tout adonnées aus bonnes lettres, ma seur, et il en prendra bien a nous et a nos sujets. A Dieu. De Compienne, 25. d'Aoust. 1554.

XXIII.

CARNEADES disoit, que les enfans des Rois n'apprenoient rien bien qu'a picquer un cheval : pour ce qu'en toutes autres choses chacun les flatte. Mais le cheval, par ce que n'entend si c'est un povre ou un riche qui est sur lui, un prince ou une personne privée, il jecte bas quicunque ne se scait bien tenir. Et maintenant encore voit-on ceci estre faict en beaucoup d'endroicts. Car ni les nourrices seullement, ni les compagnons ou serviteurs des princes les flattent, mais aussi et le gouverneur, et le precepteur, ne regardant à ce qu'ils laissent le prince meilleur, mais qu'ils s'en allent bien riches. O chose miserable, et la cause que tant le povre peuple souffre, c'est que les princes ne sont bien apprins. Qui me fait vous prier, mon oncle, de recommander tousjours ma jeunesse a ceux qui plus aiment la vertu que les biens. 26. d'Aoust.

sint exemplum virtutis. Sic faciat domi ut a nemine
possit reprehendi. Et non videatur foris nisi faciens
vel cogitans publicam utilitatem. Tum debet curare
maxime ut sermo illius nihil sapiat nisi virtutem. Id
quod non potest fieri sine doctrina. Simus ergo
omnino deditæ bonis literis, soror, et præclare nobis-
cum et subditis agetur. Vale.

XXIII.

M. SC. R. AVUNCULO A LOTHARINGIA S. P. D.

CARNEADES dicebat, spectatissime avuncule, liberos
Regum nihil recte discere præter artem equitandi, quia
in omnibus rebus unusquisque illis assentatur. Sed
æqus, quia non inteligit si sit pauper vel dives qui
insidet, princeps an privatus, excutit a tergo quicunque
non bene insiderit. Nunc etiam hoc videmus fieri
multis in locis ; nam nec nutrices solum nec comites et
ministri principum adulantur illis, sed etiam modera-
tores et præceptores : non advertentes si relinquant
principem meliorem, modo illi abeant locupletiores.
O rem miserrimam. Ea certe causa est cur subditi
omnes patiantur, nam principes non emendantur.
Quare te deprecor, mi avuncule, ut me semper com-
mendes ijs qui ante divitias virtutem amant. Vale.

XXIV.

La cause pour quoi tant de gens errent aujourdhui en l'ecriture saincte c'est qui ne la manient avec un cueur pur et net. Car Dieu ne donne l'intelligence de ses secres, si non aux innocens et gens de bien. Et n'est facile a tous de conoitre que c'est que de Dieu, comme mieux le scavés que moi. J'ai leu que Simonides, interrogué de Hiero quel estoit Dieu, et que c'estoit de lui, demanda un jour pour en repondre, et quand le lendemain lui demanda reponce, il demanda de rechef deus jours. Mais quand toujours redoubloit le temps, et que Hiero lui demandoit pourquoi il faisoit cela, pour ce (dit-il) que de tant plus j'i pense, tant plus la chose me semble difficile et obscure. 29. d'Aoust.

XXV.

J'ai entendu, ma seur, qu'hier a votre lecon vous fustes opiniatre. Vous aves promis de ne le plus estre; je vous prie laisser cette coutume. Et penser que quand la princesse prend le livre entre ses mains, elle le doit prendre non pour se delecter seulement, mais pour s'en retorner meilleure de la leçon. Et la

MULTI homines errant his temporibus in scriptura sancta, mi avuncule, quod eam non legunt puro corde et mundo. Nam Deus non dat intellectum arcanorum suorum nisi innocentibus. Nec facile est omnibus Deum cognoscere, ut tu melius quam ego scis. Legi quod Simonides interrogatus ab Hierone quis esset Deus, postulavit unum diem ut responderet. Et quando postridie quæret idem, petiit iterum.duos dies. Quumque sæpius duplicaret numerum dierum petijt Hiero cur id faceret. Quia, inquit, quanto diutius cogito, tanto res est mihi obscurior. Vale. 3. Cal. Sept.

XXV.

M. SC. R. ELI. SORORI S. P. D.

INTELLEXI, soror, quod heri in tua lectione fuisti pertinax. Promisisti te non amplius esse. Te deprecor ut relinquas istam consuetudinem, et cogites quod quum princeps accipit librum, sumere debet non solum ut delectetur, sed ut discedat melior a lectione, et major pars bonitatis est velle bonum fieri, quod

fait. Que si vous le voules, certainement vous le poves, et a fin que bien tost aies l'esprit digne de princesse, pensés que ceux qui vous reprennent, et amonestent librement, sont ceus qui vous aiment le plus. Pour quoi acoutumes vous a ceus la, et les aimes aussi. A Villiers Cotterets. 8. de Septembre.

XXVI.

A FIN que puissies repondre a ces beaus deviseurs qui disoient hier que c'est affaire aus femmes a ne rien scavoir : je vous vueil bien dire, ma seur, qu'une femme de votre nom a esté si scavante qu'elle leur eut bien repondu si elle i eut esté. C'est Elizabet abbesse d'Allemaigne, laquelle a ecrit beaucoup de belles oraisons aus seurs de son couvent, et un œuvre des chemins par lesquels on va a Dieu. Themistoclea, seur de Pythagoras, estoit si docte, qu'en plusieurs lieus il a use des opinions d'icelles. Et afin que vous aiés de quoi satisfaire a tels messieurs, je vous en apprendrai un grand nombre d'autres. Adieu, et celle qui vous aime, ma seur, aimes la beaucoup aussi. A Villiers Cotterets. 10. de Septembre.

dant errata tua et libere te docent esse qui te plurimum
amant. Quare et illos assuescito amare. Vale.

XXVI.

M. SC. R. EL. SORORI S. P. D.

Uᴛ possis respondere bellis istis blateronibus qui heri
dicebant esse fœminarum nihil sapere. Volo tibi
dicere, soror, fœminam tui nominis adeò sapientem
fuisse ut bene respondisset illis si adfuisset. Est
Elizabeta abbatissa Germanica, quæ scripsit plures
orationes ad sorores sui conventus, et opus de vijs
quibus itur ad superos. Themistoclea soror Pythagoræ ita docta erat, ut pluribus in locis usus sit illius
opinionibus. Et ut habeas unde satisfacias ijs homunculis, te docebo magnum alliarum numerum. Vale, et
illam quæ te plurimum amat, soror, ama. Vale iterum.
10. Sept.

D

Vous dirés encores a ces babillars qu'il i a eu trois Corrinnes tres doctes, des quelles celle qui estoit de Thebes a écrit cinq livres d'epigrammes, et cinq fois vainquit Pindare, prince de poètes lyriques. Erinne en langue dorique composa un poeme de trois cents vers, et beaucoup d'autres epigrammes. Et disent que ses carmes approchoient de la gravité, et majesté d'Homère. Elle fut morte en l'age de .19. ans. Sappho a esté admirable en tout genre de carmes. Polla, comme on dit, femme de Lucain, a esté de si grande doctrine, qu'elle a aidé a son mari a corriger les trois premiers livres de Pharsale. Aspasia a enseigné la rhétorique, et a esté maitresse de Periclès, et sa femme. Je vous en nommerai demain plusieurs autres. Adieu. 11. de Septembre.

XXVIII.

CLEOBULINE, fille de Cléobule, qui fut un des sept sages de Grece, a ecrit beaucoup de beaus enigmes en vers exametres. Cornificia, seur de Cornificius, poete, a fait des epigrammes très elegans. Cornelie, femme

DICES adhuc illis homunculis futilibus tres fuisse Corinnas doctissimas, quarum quæ erat Thebana scripsit quinque libros epigrammatum, et vicit quinquies Pindarum principem poetarum lyricorum. Erinna lingua Dorica composuit poema trecentis versibus et alia epigrammata. Et ferunt quod illius carmina accedebant ad gravitatem Homeri. Mortua est annos nata 19. Sappho fuit admirabilis in omnibus generibus carminum. Polla, ut aiunt, uxor Lucani, fuit tanta doctrina ut adiuverit maritum in coripiendis tribus primis libris Pharsaliæ. Aspasia docuit rhetoricen, fuit magistra Periclis, et tandem uxor. Cras numerabo alias quam plurimas. Vale. 11. Septemb.

XXVIII.

M. SC. R. EL. SORORI S. P. D.

CLEOBULINA, filia Cleobuli, qui fuit unus septem sapientum Græciæ, scripsit plura pulcra ænigmata versibus exametris. Cornificia, soror Cornificij poetæ, composuit epigrammata elegantissima. Cornelia, uxor

epitres bien latinement écrites, et d'elle est sortie l'eloquence de ses enfans. La fille de Lælius en parlant exprimoit l'eloquence de son père; et l'oraison de la fille d'Hortense qu'elle fit devant les triumvirs, temoigne qu'elle estoit très eloquente. Retenés diligemment toutes celles que je vous nomme, afin de povoir repondre a tous ceus qui tant meprisent notre sexe, disant n'estre affaire aus femmes d'apprendre la langue latine.

XXIX.

Vous leur dires encores (ma seur) qu'Anastase, disciple de Chrysogone martyr, a esté et bien docté et bien saincte. Elle fut brulée pour ce qu'elle ministroit aus saincts. Damophila, grecque, ecrivit les louanges de Diane et quelques poesies d'amours. Hypathia, femme du philosophe Isidore, a composé de l'astronomie, et a montré en Alexandrie plusieurs disciplines d'une si grande dexterité d'esprit, que les echoliers venoient à elle de tous costés. Leontia, fillette grecque, a tant poursuit les disciplines de philosophie, qu'elle n'a redouté avec une grande louange écrire contre Theophraste philosophe très renommé. Praxilla a

scriptas, et ab illa effluxit eloquentia filiorum. Filia
Lælij exprimebat loquendo eloquentiam patris. Et
oratio Hortensiæ, Hortensij filiæ, quam habuit ante
triumviros, testatur quod erat elegantissima. Manda
memoriæ diligenter omnes quas numerabo, ut possis
respondere ijs, qui spernunt nostrum sexum, quique
dicunt non esse officium fœminæ discere linguam la-
tinam. Vale. 12. Septem.

XXIX.

M. SC. R. EL. SORORI S. P. D.

ILLIS itaque dices, soror, quod Anastasia, discipula
Chrysogoni martyris, fuit multum et docta et pia.
Cremata est quia ministrabat sanctis. Damophila
Græca scripsit laudes Dianæ et quædam poematæ amoris.
Hypathia, uxor philosophi Isidori, composuit in astro-
nomiam et docuit in Alexandria plures disciplinas
tanta dexteritate ingenij ut discipuli avvolabant undique
ad illam. Leontia, puela græca, adeo prosecuta est
disciplinas philosophicas ut non dubitaverit cum magna
laude scribere in Theophrastum philosophum optimum.
Praxilla excelluit multum in omne arte poetica. Quia

PHEMONOE est du nombre de ces doctes et sages
femmes. Sosipatra a esté poète, et pleine de tant de
disciplines, qu'on pensoit qu'elle eut esté nourrie de
quelques dieus. Theano fut une femme excellente
en vers lyriques. Une autre de ce mesme nom a este
femme pythagoriaine, laquelle a ecrit en philosophie
des commentaires de vertu, et des poesies et apoph-
thegmes aussi. Zenobia, royne des Palmyriains, a
esté scavante en la langue grecque et egiptienne, et
non ignorante en la latine. Elle a enseigné les lettres
a deus enfans qu'elle avoit. Et souvent fait des
oraisons a ses gendarmes lesquelles aiant l'armet en
teste elle recitoit. Alpaides, vierge, a esté si amie
de la religion, qu'elle a du ciel merité comprendre le
sens de la Bible, et de l'ecriture saincte. C'est aujourd'-
hui la feste de la ste crois, en laquelle pour nostre
salut a pendu l'eternel Jesuschrist fils du Dieu eternel.
Je voi au parc pour un petit recréer mon entendement,
qui est cause que je fai ici fin.

XXX.

M. SC. R. EL. SORORI S. P. D.

PHEMONOE ascribitur numero istarum doctarum et sapientum fœminarum. Sosipatra fuit vates et plena tantis disciplinas *(sic)*, ut crediderint omnes eam fuisse educatam a quibusdam numinibus. Theano excelluit apud Locros versibus lyricis. Altera ejusdem nominis fuit pythagorica, quæ scripsit in philosophiam commentarios de virtute, poemata quoque et apopthegmata. Zenobia regina Palmireorum fuit eruditissima sermonis græci, ægiptij, et non ignara latini. Erudijt filios duos quos habebat literis. Et plerunque habuit orationes apud suos milites quas galatea *(for* galeata) recitabat. Alpaides virgo fuit adeo religionis amica, ut meruerit celitus percipere sensum bibliorum, et scripturæ sacræ. Hodie est festus dies sanctæ crucis, in qua pro nostra salute pependit æternus Jesus Christus filius æterni patris. Dicedo in arbustum ut recreem meum ingenium, quare finem scribendi facio. Vale. 14. Septemb.

DELBORA, femme de la lignée d'Effrain, estoit docte,
et devinoit les choses futures. Lastemia et Axiothea
(comme temoigne Plutarque) ont esté disciples de
Platon, et a fin qu'elles eussent plus de moien de con-
verser cà et là avec les gens scavans, elles entroient
a l'echolle en habit d'homme. Michale très doctement
a enseigné a Thessale le remède d'amours. Diotima
et Aspasia ont tant profité en philosophie, que l'une, a
scavoir Diotima, Socrates, prince des philosophes, n'a
eu honte appeller sa maitresse, ni d'aller aus leçons de
l'autre, comme Platon a laissé par ecrit. Lactantius
dit que Themiste devant tout autre a esté excellente
en philosophie. Le roi m'a donné congé de prendre
un daim au parc avec ma dame de Castres, dont je
n'ai loisir vous faire plus longue lettre. 15. Sept.

ARETE est pervenue a si grande doctrine, qu'après
que son père Aristippe fut mort, elle tint son echole
en philosophie, et eut plusieurs auditeurs. Dama,
fille de Pythagoras, avoit l'esprit si grand en philoso-

DELBORA, mulier ex tribu Effrain, erat peritissima, quæ prædicebat res futuras. Lastemia et Axiothea, ut testatur Plutarcus, fuerunt discipulæ Platonis, et ut facilius cum hominibus doctioribus versarentur, ingrediebantur scholas cum habitu virili. Michale doctissima docuit apud Thessalos remedium amoris. Diothima et Aspasia adeo in philosophia profecerunt ut Socrates princeps philosophorum non veritus sit alteram, videlicet Diotimam, nominare magistram, et alterius lectionibus interesse, ut Plato scriptum reliquit. Lactantius dicit Themistem ante omnes alias fuisse excellentiorem in philosophia. Rex mihi permisit accipere damam in Theriotrophio; eo venatum cum domina a Castris, unde non licet per otium plura scribere. Vale.

ARETE pervenit ad tam maximam doctrinam, ut patre Aristippo mortuo rexerit scholas in philosophia, habuitque plures auditores. Dama filia Pythagoræ prædita erat ingenio philosophiæ dedito, ut exposuerit patris

en philosophie. On dit que Musca a esté poëte lyrique, et a ecrit plusieurs epigrammes. Carixena a fait aussi beaucoup de vers très elegans. Ma lettre ne sera plus longue, ma seur, pour ce que n'estes encores asses bien guerie. Si je ne vous fu hier voir, le medecin en est cause, qui ne le voulut, pour ce qu'avés prins medecine. 18. Sept.

XXXIII.

On loue aussi Mæro pour une hynne qu'elle a faite a la louange de Neptune. Agallis de Corce *(sic)* a esté fort illustre en grammaire, et Telesilla en poesie, laquelle loue grandement Pausanias, et lui fut erigée une statue en l'insule d'Argos, devant le temple de Venus. Hipparchia, femme grecque, a semblablement esté merveilleuse aus disciplines de philosophie. Je ne vous en nommerai d'autres pour le present, pour ce qui faut que j'alle voir le roi qui print au soir des pillules. Je n'eu loisir de vous visiter hier, je vous prie, ma seur, de me pardonner. 20. Sept.

lyricam, quæ scripsit plura epigrammata: Charixena fecit etiam plures elegantissimos versus. Non erit æpistola mea longior, suavissima soror, quia nondum satis convalescis. Si te non viserim heri, medicus in causa est, noluit enim propterea quod acceperas medicinam. Vale.

XXXIII.

M. SC. R. EL. SORORI S. P. D.

LAUDATUR etiam Mæro hymno condito in laudem Neptuni. Agallis Corcirea fuit illustrissima in arte grammatica. Telesilla in poetica quam Pausanias valde celebrat, erecta fuit illi statua apud Argos ante templum Veneris. Hipparchia, mulier Græca, similiter excelluit in disciplinis philosophicis. Nullas numerabo alias in præsentia, quia oportet me ire ad regem, qui sero accepit catapotia. Non licuit per otium invisere te heri, quare te oratum velim, soror, ut mihi parcas. Vale.

CASSANDRE, fille de Priam, a esté prophète et de doctrine
tres acomplie, et de ses ennemis honorée d'un temple en
Lacedemone. Statius Papinius eut une femme nommée
Claudia d'un esprit tres grand et admirable doctrine.
Eudoxia, femme de Theodore le plus jeune, outre une
grande beauté et une singulière pudicité, a tant excellé aus lettres qu'elle a mis en lumière un beau
livre. Istrina, reyne des Scythes, temoin Herodote, a
enseigné les lettres grecques a Syle son fils. C'est
asses pour maintenant. Il faut ouir que demande
Philodoxus a Simbulus en Erasme. Adieu. 22. Septembre.

POLITIEN loue grandement Cassandre Fidele, fille
venitiaine, laquelle il dit avoir manié le livre au lieu
de la laine, la plume pour le fuseau, et le style pour
l'éguille. De laquelle au commencement de quelque
epitre il parle ainsi: O vierge, l'honneur d'Italie,
quelle grace te pui-je rendre de quoi tu ne dedaignes
m'honorer de tes lettres. Proba Valeria, fillette

Cassandra filia Priami fuit vates et illustris doctrina, et apud hostes templo insignita in Lacedemone. Statius Papinius habuit uxorem nomine Claudiam, magno ingenio, et non vulgari doctrina præditam. Eudoxia, uxor Theodori junioris, præter egregiam formam, et singularem pudicitiam, ita excelluit literis, ut librum quendam emiserit in lucem. Istrina, regina Scytharum, ut testis est Herodotus, docuit Sylem filium literas Græcas. Hæc hactenus, audiamus quid velit Philodoxus Simbulo apud Erasmum. Vale. 22. Septembris.

XXXV.

M. SC. R. EL. SORORI S. P. D.

Politianus laudat mirum in modum Cassandram Fidelem filiam Venetianam, quam dicit tractasse librum pro lana, pennam pro fuso, et stylum pro acu. De qua in principio cujusdam epistolæ ita loquitur. O virgo decus Italiæ, quales gratias possim tibi reddere, quod non dedigneris me honorare tuis literis. Proba Valeria puella Romana fuit excellentissima, cum græcis

de vous aller voir, ma seur, pour ce qu'elle pense que
vous avés la rougeolle, de quoi je suis bien fort marrie.
Je vous prie me mander comme vous portés. 23. Septembre.

XXXVI.

BAPTISTE premiere fille du prince Mal[at]este, a souvent disputé contre gens des plus doctes, avec une
très grand louange, et a ecrit des livres de la fragilité
humaine et de la vraie religion. Isota, fille de Veronne,
a fait grande profession de philosophie et a quelque
fois ecrit a pape Nicolas cinquiesme, et Pie second de
ce nom. Elle a encor ecrit un dialogue, auquel elle
dispute lequel a le plus offensé, Adam ou Eve: aus
quelles louanges des lettres elle a adjoutté le veu de
perpetuelle virginité. A Dieu, ma seur, bien aimée.
A Paris, 12. d'Octobre 1554.

XXXVII.

[*The French has*

ne te viserem, soror, quod putet te laborare pustulis sive boa. Qua de re dolenter fero, atque unice te oro mihi significes ut valeas. Vale.

XXXVI.

MA. SC. R. ELIZA. SORORI S. P. D.

BAPTISTA, prima Malatestæ Pisauriensis principis filia, sæpe magna sui laude disputavit cum viris doctissimis, et scripsit libros de humana fragilitate, et de vera religione. Isota Navarola Veronensis professa est philosophiam, et quandoque scripsit ad Nicolaum quintum et Pium secundum, pontifices. Conscripsit etiam dialogum quo disputatur uter peccaverit gravius, Adam, an Eva, quibus laudibus adjecit virginitatis votum perpetuum. Vale, amica summa mea et soror. Lutetiæ, 12. Octobris.

XXXVII.

M. SC. R. EL. SORORI S. P. D.

MINERVA, prima Jovis filia, non propter aliud relata est in numerum deorum, nisi quia docta esset in

XXXVIII.

CATHERINE, fille du roi d'Alexandrie, a esté si bien apprise aus saintes lettres, et par son labeur, et par inspiration divine, qu'elle a vaincu plusieurs hommes doctes appellés de son père pour lui persuader l'idolatrie, et [faire quitter] la religion d'un seul Dieu. Fabiole, femme romaine, a d'un cueur si grand ambrassé les sainctes lettres, et lisoit si souvent les propheties, evangiles, et autres bonnes leçons, qu'elle a grandement augmenté l'amour de la religion. Sainct Hierome a souvent ecrit a Marcelle romaine, pour ce qu'elle scavoit fort bien les lettres grecques, et lui a dedié le livre qu'il a fait du mepris du monde, de notre foi, et de la doctrine des heretiques, du blaspheme contre le St. Esprit, et plusieurs autres choses. Il faut que j'alle à vespre avec la roine, qui me garde vous faire plus longue lettre. A Paris.

claruit.   Nicostrata græcas literas inpense dicta
[This theme is left unfinished.]

M. SC. R. EL. SORORI S. P. D.

CATHARINA, regis Alexandriæ filia, adeo sacris literis imbuta fuit, partim suo labore, partim afflatu divini spiritus, ut vicerit plures doctissimos viros vocatos a patre ad persuadendam idolatriam, et fugiendam unius Dei religionem. Fabiola, mulier Romana, tanto studio amplexa est sanctas literas, et revolvebat prophetias, evangelia, et alias bonas lectiones, ut auxerit vehementer amorem religionis.   Divus Hieronimus sæpe scripsit Marcellæ Romanæ propter sacras literas quas egregie callebat, et ad eam scripsit librum quem fecit de contemptu mundi, de nostra fide, de doctrina hereticorum, de blasphemia in spiritum sanctum, et alia id genus permulta.   Oportet me interesse vesperis cum Regina, quare addam finem meis literis. Lutetiæ. 28. Octob.   Vale.

E

XXXIX.

EUSTOCHIUM, fille de Paule femme romaine, a excellé aus etudes de lettres hébraiques, greques, et latines : tant que de son temps elle fut appellée nouveau monstre du monde. Elle se voua, et s'addonna du tout aus letres sainctes, de quoi St. Hierome l'aima, et loua fort. Genebria, femme de la nation de Veronne du temps de pape Pie 2. par sa grande erudition se rendit immortelle. Elle a écrit des epitres pleines de grande doctrine.

XL.

CONSTANTIA, femme d'Alexandre Sforce, est mise au nombre des femmes excellentes en doctrine. Laquelle dès son enfance a estudié aus bonnes disciplines, de sorte que promptement sans y avoir pensé elle scavoit parler elegamment. Elle avoit tousjours aus mains les œuvres de St. Hierome, de St. Ambroise, de St. Gregoire, Cicero, et Lactance. Promptement elle ecrivoit des carmes tres elegans, ce qu'on disoit qu'elle avoit appris sans maitre. Elle eut une fille nommée Baptiste, d'une si grande doctrine qu'elle epouvantoit

XXXIX.

M. R. SC. EI.. SORORI S. P. D.

Eustochium, filia Paulæ mulieris Romanæ, excelluit
studijs literarum hebraicarum, græcarum et latinarum,
adeo ut suo tempore appellata fuerit novum monstrum
totius mundi. Vovit et addixit se omnino sacris literis,
quapropter divus Hieronimus eam et amavit et maxime
laudavit. Genebria, mulier natione Veronensis tempore pontificis Pij. 2. meruit immortale nomen incredi-
bili sua eruditione. Scripsit epistolas maxima doctrina plenas.

XL.

M. SC. R. EI.. SORORI S. P. D.

Constantia, uxor Alexandri Sfortiæ, ascribitur numero feminarum excellentium doctrina. Quæ ab
infantia studuit bonis disciplinis, ita ut imparata poterat
loqui eleganter. Semper habebat in manibus opus Sti.
Hieronimi, Ambrosij, Gregorij, Ciceronis, et Lactancij.
Scribebat ex tempore (*sic*) carmina elegantissima.
Id quod fertur didiscisse sine præceptore. Habuit
filiam, nomine Baptistam, tanta doctrina, ut terreret
doctiores eloquentia. Manda memoriæ id quod ad te

vous ai ecrit de toutes ces femmes, ma seur, et a leur
exemple mettons peine d'apprendre les bonnes lettres,
lesquelles, ainsi comme elles, nous rendront immor-
telles a jamais.

XLI.

Il ne faut pas que vous soiés marrie, si toutes les fois
que vous faillés, vous estes reprise. Car en toute
institution, et mesmement en celle du prince, telle
diligence y doit estre mise que la severité du precepteur
corrige et emende les follies d'icelui. Et pour ce n'en
aimés moins ceux qui vous tensent : mais au contraire,
estimes fideles non ceus qui louent tout ce que vous
faites et dites, mais ceus qui quand vous faillés vous
reprennent aprement. Ceus la, ma dame, sont les
vrais et plus seurs amis du Prince. Adieu. De notre
Bibliotheque a St. Germain, ce 23. Novembre.

XLII.

Il ne nous faut perdre le courage, ma seur, si la vertu
et le scavoir sont longs a apprendre, car toutes choses

XLI.

Non est quod egre feras, hera, si quoties erras, repre-
henderis. Nam in omni istitutione *(sic)*, et maxime in
ea quæ pertinet ad principem, ea adhibenda est diligentia, ut severitas præceptoris corrigat et emendet
illius laciviam *(sic)*. Quare ne illos minus ama qui te
objurgant : sed contra existima eos esse fideles, non
qui laudant quicquid dixeris fecerisve, sed qui te
erantem increpant. Illi, hera, veri sunt amici principis.
Vale. Ex nostra biblioteca, apud Stm. Germanum.
23. Novembris.

XLII.

M. SC. R. ELIZABETÆ SO. S. P. D.

Non oportet nos despondere animum, soror, si virtus
et eruditio discantur cum longo tempore. Nam ea

et que Zeuxis [restoit] trop long temps sur l'œuvre. Mais Zeuxis repondit, Je mets long temps a paindre, car je pain pour jamais. Les choses si tost nées perissent bien soudainement, et celles qui sont long temps elaborées durent un long age. La bête croit bien tost, et le buis petit a petit : regardés, ma seur, lequel dure plus. Prenés donc courage, ma joie, la vertu est eternelle. A St. Germain. 24. Novembre. 1554.

.

XLIII.

Agesilaus interrogué par quel moien povoit acquerir honneste renommée : Si parle, repondit-il, ce qui est très bon, et fait ce qui est très honneste. Socrates respondit ainsi a celui qui demandoit le mesme, Si tu estudies, dit-il, a estre tel que tu veus estre veu. Car la gloire acquise par fards, n'est vraie gloire et ne dure guères. Gardons nous donc, ma seur, ni en jeu ni a bon esciant de dire ni faire que choses bonnes. A Dieu.

pictor, sese jactabat de celeritate pingendi, quod
Zeuxis immoraretur operi. At Zeuxis respondit,
diu pingo, sed pingo æternitati. Res tam subito natæ,
pereunt cito, et illæ quæ diu sunt elaboratæ, durant
per longam ætatem. Beta statim crescit, et buxus
paulatim. Vide, soror, utrum plus durat. Sis animo
forti, mea voluptas unica, virtus æterna manebit.
Apud St. Germanum. 24. Novembris. Vale.

XLIII.

M. SC. R. EL. SORORI S. P. D.

AGESILAUS interrogatus qua ratione quisque posset
assequi honestam famam : Si loquatur, inquit, id quod
optimum sit, et fecerit quod honestissimum. Socrates
itidem respondit idem petenti, si tu studeas esse talis,
qualis haberi velis. Nam gloria parta fucis, non est
vera gloria, nec diuturna. Curemus igitur, soror, ne
ioco, vel serio, quid dicamus faciamusve, nisi quod
optimum sit. Vale. 27. Novembris.

Je lisoi au soir, un peu devant que m'endormir, une sentence d'Antalcidas digne d'estre apprise d'un chacun et mesmement d'un prince. Icelui, interrogué comment quelcun pourroit plaire aus hommes : Si parle, dit-il, a eux gratieusement, et leur donne choses utiles. Il vous apprent (mes dames) qu'en vos propos il i ait grand douceur de paroles, et que soiés liberales, donnant choses qui apportent grand profit a ceus aus quels vous donnerés. 27. Novembre.

Quand quelque fois Denis entra en la chambre de son fils, et apperceut un si grand monceau de vases d'or et d'argent, s'écriant, N'as-tu, dit-il, l'entendement royal, que tu n'as fait quelque ami de tant de pots que je t'ai donnés ? Voulant dire que sans la benevolence des citoiens le royaume ne se peut acquérir ni estre gardé. Et n'i a rien qui plus concilie l'amitié et benevolence que liberalité. Mais le jeune enfant, ignorant du maniment de choses, pensoit estre plus grand heur avoir de l'argent que des amis. Fuions l'avarice, ma seur, car elle est du tout indigne de la nature du prince.

Heri legebam paulo ante quam discederem cubitum, Alcidæ (*sic*) sententiam dignam quæ discatur ab unoquoque, et a principe maxime. Is interrogatus quomodo quisque posset hominibus placere : Si loquatur, inquit, illis jucundissime, et det illis utilissima. Vos docet, heræ suavissimæ meæ, ut in colloquijs vestris sit sermonis comitas maxima, tam ut sitis liberale dando quæ adferant utilitatem ijs quibus dederitis. Bene valete. 27. Novembris.

XLV.

M. SC. R. ELI. SORORI S. P. D.

Quum aliquando Dionisius ingrederetur cubiculum filij, et videret magnam vim poculorum aureorum et argnteorum *(sic)*, exclamans, Non habes, inquit, regium animum, qui nullum feceris amicum ex tantis poculis quæ dedi tibi? Sentiens sine benevolentia civium regium non posse parari, nec servari. Nihil est quod plus conciliet amicitiam et benevolentiam quam liberalitas. Sed juvenis imperitus rerum putabat esse felicius habere argentum quam amicos. Fugiamus avvaritiam, soror, nam indigna est omnino natura principis. Vale. 28. Novembris.

XLVI.

ARISTODEMUS, un des grands amis d'Antigonus roi de Macédone, encores qui fut fils d'un cuisinier, lui persuadoit de retraindre sa dépence et ses liberalités. Tes paroles, dit-il, Aristodeme, sentent la saulce. Montrant la chicheté, si elle estoit aus cuisiniers, ne devoir estre aus rois. Et que par tel conseil il lui souvenoit de quel pere il estoit né, et non de qui il estoit ami. Antigone montroit par cela ce que disoit Artoxerces fils de Xerces; a scavoir, qu'il est plus digne a un prince d'augmenter les honneurs et richesses de ceus aus quels ils commandent, que les diminuer.

XLVII.

CETTE histoire, ma seur, n'est de moindre dignité et utilité que celle que je vous contoi hier. Perillus, un des amis d'Alexandre, lui demanda douaire pour ses filles. Le roi commanda qu'il prist cinquante talents. Perillus repondit que dix seroient assés. C'est assés a toi, dit Alexandre, d'en recevoir autant, mais a moi non de n'en donner qu'autant. O liberalité digne d'un vrai prince. A Dieu, ma seur, je ne vous ferai plus longue lettre, par ce que j'ai mal aus dents. A St. Germain.

Quum Aristodemus unus ex numero amicorum Anti-
goni Regis Macedoniæ, quamvis esset prognatus à
coquo, persuaderet regi detrahere impendia et largitiones,
Tua verba, inquit, Aristodeme, ius olent: demonstrans
avaritiam esse coquorum, non regum, et tali consilio
ind[i]care à quo patre natus esset, non cujus erat
amicus. Antigonus hoc dicto demonstrabat, id quod
Artoxerces filius Xercis dicebat, videlicet dignius esse
principi augere honores, et divitias eorum, quibus
imperat, quam minuere. Vale. 4. Calend. Decemb.
apud St. Germanum.

Hæc historia non est indignior nec inutilior illa quam
tibi recitabam heri. Perillus, unus amicorum Alexandri, ab Alexandro petijt dotem pro suis filiabus.
Rex jussit ut acciperet quinquaginta talenta. Perillus
respondit decem satis esse. Sufficeret tibi, inquit
Alexander, tantum accipere, sed mihi non satis est
tantum dare. O liberalitatem dignam vero principe.
Vale, soror dilectissima mea, non possum longiorem
facere epistolam, quia laboro dentibus. Apud St.
Germanum. 3. cal. Decemb.

XLVIII.

Je trouve la liberalité d'Alexandre si emerveillable
que je ne me puis tenir vous en parler. Quand quelque fois Xenocrates philosophe refusa cinquante talens
qui lui envoia en don, disant qu'il n'en avoit que faire,
lui demanda s'il avoit point d'amis qui en eussent
besoin. A grand peine les richesses de Darius (dist
le roi) m'ont-elles suffit pour mes amis.

XLIX.

Je vous raconterai (ma seur) une liberalité plus grande
que toutes les autres. Anaxarchus philosophe vint au
roy Alexandre pour ce qui scavoit bien qu'il estoit
liberal, et qu'il aimoit fort les lettres, et lui demanda
argent pour bastir un college. Le roy commanda a
son tresorier qui donnast au philosophe ce qu'il
demanderoit. Le tresorier, estonné de la demande du
philosophe, remontra au roy qu'il demandoit cents
talents. Il fait bien, dit-il, sachant qu' Alexandre en
peut et veut autant donner. Voiant ce roy avoir
acquis une si grande renommée par liberalité, je suis
marrie que je n'ai de quoi je puisse faire paroitre ma
volonté.

TANTA mihi videtur liberalitas regis Alexandri ut non possum quin tibi iterum loquar de illo. Quum aliquoties Xenocrates philosophus recusavit quinquaginta talenta quæ misit illi dono, dicens non esse illi opus : Petijt si non haberet amicos quibus esset opus. Vix, inquit, opes Darij mihi suffecerunt in meos amicos. Vale. Apud St. Germanum. Decembris.

HANC etiam tibibi (*sic*) recitabo liberalitatem majorem omnibus alijs. Anaxarchus philosophus venit ad regem Alexandrum, quod sciret eum esse liberalem et amare literas, et petiit ab eo argentum ut gymnasium ædificaret. Rex imperavit quæstori ut daret philosopho id quod peteret. Quæstor turbatus petitione philosophi indicavit Regi illum petere centum talenta. Bene facit, inquit, scit enim Alexandrum et posse et velle tantum dare. Quare videns hunc Regem tantam acquisisse famam liberalitate, dolet mihi quod non habeam unde possim patefacere meum beneficentissimum animum. Decembris.

L.

JE vous prie, ma seur, vouloir entendre la reponce que fit ce tres liberal roy Alexandre. Interrogué où il mettroit tous ses tresors, Devers mes amis, dit-il; signifiant, que les richesses ne peuvent estre mises plus seurement. Car quand la chose et le temps le requiert, elles reviennent à nous avec usure. Apprenons, ma seur, qu'il est plus honneste donner que prendre, et pensons que Dieu ne nous a donné tant de richesses pour les garder en un monseau, mais pour les departir a ceux qui en ont besoin.

LI.

JE me suis ebahi ce matin, ma seur, de voir les anciens ethniques, privés de la cognoissance de notre foi, estre plus sages que nous. Je lisoi que Socrates disoit qui ne failloit demander a Dieu que sa grâce, reprenant ceux qui demandent une femme bien douée, des biens, des honneurs, des roiaumes, longue vie, comme voulant enseigner a Dieu ce qu'il faut faire. Ne faisons pas ainsi, ma seur, car Dieu scait mieux ce qui nous est bon, et ce qui nous est mauvais que nous mesme.

L.

M. SC. R. EL. SORORI S. P. D.

ORO te, soror, ut intelligas quid responderit liberalissimus rex Alexander. Interrogatus ubi reconderet suos thesauros, Apud meos amicos, inquit, significans quod opes non possunt reponi tutius. Nam cum res et tempus postulant, redeunt ad nos cum fœnore. Discamus, soror, quod est fœlicius dare quam accipere. Et putemus Deum non nobis dedisse tantas opes ut cumulatim servaremus; sit ut daremus illis quibus opus est. Vale. 11. Decembris.

LI.

M. SC. R. EL. SORORI S. P. D.

MIRABAR hodie, soror, veteres ethnicos privatos cognitione nostræ fidei esse sapientiores nobis ipsis. Legebam Socratem dicere non oportere nihil a Deo petere, præter suam sanctissimam gratiam, obiurgantem eos qui petunt uxorem bene dotatam, opes, honores, regna, longuam (*sic*) vitam: tanquam volentes Deum docere quid oporteat facere. Ne ita faciamus, soror, nam Deus optimus maximus melius scit quid nobis optimum sit et quod opessimum (*sic*), quam nos ipsi. Vale.

La coutume des Lacedémoniens estoit que le plus viel montroit la porte a tous ceus qui entroient aus banquets, disant, Qu'une seule parole ne resorte par la. Les admonestant qu'il ne failloit rien reporter, si librement il estoit dit quelque chose au banquet. Et institua cette coutume Lycurgus. Fuions donc les raporteurs et les flateurs, ma seur, imitant Alexandre, envers lequel quand on accusoit quelq'un, il etoupoit l'une de ses oreilles. Interrogué pour quoi il faisoit cela, je garde, disoit-il, l'autre entiere a celui qu'on acuse.

Quand je lisoi les beaus faicts d'Alexandre, le plus grand que fut jamais aus armes, j'ai noté, Monsr·, qui n'aimoit rien tant que les lettres. Car quand on lui porta un petit coffret, si beau que rien ne se trouvoit plus excellent entre les richesses de Darius, et qu'on demandoit a quel usage il seroit destiné, les uns disant d'un, les autres d'autre: Il lui sera donné Homère a garder, dit-il; voulant dire qu'il n'estoit tresor plus grand que cela. Ce qu'il approuva une

LII.

M. SC. R. EL. SORORI S. P. D.

CONSUETUDO Lacedemoniorum erat, ut is qui senior, ostenderet fores illis omnibus qui ingrediebantur convivia, inquiens, ne quis sermo per has fores egrediatur. Admonens eos nihil effutiendum esse, si quid liberius diceretur in convivio. Hunc morem institutur Lycurgus. Fugiamus igitur adulatores, et linguaces, soror, imitantes Alexandrum, apud quem, cum aliquis accusabatur, occludebat alteram aurem. Interogatus cur hoc faceret, Servo, dicebat, alteram integram illi qui accusatur. Vale.

LIII.

M. DEI GRATIA SCOTORUM REGINA FRANCISCO DELPHINO S. P. D.

QUUM legerem pulchra facinora Alexandri, maioris quam qui unquam fuerit in armis hoc unum notavi (princeps illustrissime), eum nihil æque ac literas amare. Nam cum tulissent illi scriniolum adeo pulcrum ut nihil pulcrius inter opes Darij, et petiissent in quem usum destinandum esset: alijs aliud suadentibus dabitur huic servandus Homerus, inquit, signifigans se nihil potius amare, nec u[l]lum eo thesaurum præciosiorem. Id quod alias probavit, quum quidam gaudio gestiens

F

neureusement advenue. Que m'annonceras tu de
grand, dit-il, mon amy, si tu ne disois qu'Homere
requist [revequist]? Signifiant toute la gloire de
beaus faicts perir, si ni a un tel bon chanteur qu'a
esté Homère. Aimés doncques les lettres, Monsr,
lesquelles seullement n'augmenteront vos vertus, mais
rendront immortels vos beaus faicts. A St. Germain.
20. de Decembre.

LIV.

L'AMOUR que je vous porte, Monsr, m'a donné hardi-
esse de vous prier que le plus que vous pourrés aiés
avecques vous gens vertueux et sçavans, et que sur tout
aimés votre precepteur, a l'exemple d'Alexandre, qui
a d'une telle reverence honoré Aristote qu'il disoit ne
luy devoir moins qu'a son père. Pour ce que de son
père il en avoit pris le commancement de vivre, et de
son maître le commancement de bien vivre.

Homerum revixisse; significans gloriam pulcrorum factorum perituram, si desit talis preco, qualis Homerus fuit. Ama igitur literas, princeps illustrissime, quæ non solum augebunt tuas virtutes, sed tua pulcra facta immortalia redeunt *(for* reddunt). Vale. Apud St. Germanum. 13. Calend. Januar.

LIV.

M. DEI GRATIA SC. R. FRANCISCO DELPHINO S. P. D.

AMOR quo te unice complector, princeps illu[s]trissime, efficit ut ausim te deprecari tecum habeas quantum poteris probos et sapientes homines, et ante omnia præceptorem ames, exemplo Alexandri, qui tanta reverentia Aristotelem prosecutus est, ut diceret se non minus illi quam patri debere: quod a patre initium vivendi solum, a præceptore bene vivendi initium accipisset. Vale.

Agesilaus voiant que plusieurs estoient entachés d'avarice, avoit coutume d'admonester ses amis qui n'estudiassent tant a s'enrichir de pecunes que de force et de vertu. Pour ce qu'en vain acquiert des richesse, qui est sans les vrais biens de l'esprit. Car, ma seur, ceux-ci nous accompaignent, et font honneur après notre notre (*sic*) mort; et les autres nous trompent, et perissent en un moment. A St. Germain, 26. Decemb.

LVI.

Aristippe interrogué quelle difference il y avoit entre les doctes et les ignorans, autant qu'entre les chevaux dontés et ceus qui ne le sont point. Car tout ainsi qu'un cheval qui n'est point dressé est incommode a tout usage, pour son ignorance et ferocité : ainsi celui qui est transporté de ses affections, lesquelles la seule philosophie apprivoise, est inutile a toute coutume de la vie. A St. Germain, le jour St. Jean aprés la natiuité de Jesuchrist.

Quum videret Agsilaus *(for* Agesilaus) plures laborare pecuniæ studio, solebat admonere amicos ut ne tam pecuniis studerent ditescere, quam fortitudine et virtute. Nam frustra parat opes qui est sine veris bonis animi. Hæc nos comitantur, soror, et nobis addunt honorem : illa vero nos decipiunt, et pereunt uno momento. Vale. Apud St. Germanum.

Aristippus interrogatus quo differebant docti ab ignorantibus : quo equi domiti ab ijs qui sunt indomiti. Nam ut equs qui indomitus est incommodus est ad omnem rem ob iscitiam et ferocitatem, ita ille qui rapitur suis affectibus quos sola philosophia domat est inutilis ad omnem consuetudinem vitæ. Apud St. Germanum, die St. Ioannis a nativitate Iesu Cristi. Vale.

ARISTIPPE disoit que mieux valloit estre povre qu'estre indocte, pour ce que le povre a seulement afaire d'argent, et l'autre d'humanité. Et d'avantage celuy n'est moins homme auquel defaut argent, mais celui n'est homme auquel defaut sçavoir. Outre plus, celui qui a faute d'argent, en demande a ceux qui rencontre : et celui auquel defaut prudence, ne sollicite personne pour en avoir. Nous avons des richesses assés, ma seur, efforçons nous d'acquerir de la doctrine. A St. Germain, dernier jour de cest an 1554.

NOUS devons vouloir, ma seur très aimée, que soions, pendant que sommes jeunes, reprinses d'un chacun, afin que soions plus tost sages. Et ne nous faut dire tantost a l'un, tantost a l'autre, Quoi ? t'appartient il de me reprendre ? Diogenes disoit a Xeniades du quel il estoit acheté, combien que je soy serf, si est il necessaire que tu m'obeisses, car qui a un nautonnier, ou medecin serviteur, il est contrainct de lui obeir, s'il en veut recevoir profit. Je ne vueil oblier a vous dire que j'ai

ARISTIPPUS dicebat satius esse fieri pauperem quam indoctum : quia ille tantum eget pecunijs, hic vero humanitate. Et porro ille non minus homo est cui pecunia deest, sed non homo est cui sapientia deest. Præterea cui pecunia deest, petit ab obvijs, et ille cui prudentia deest, neminem sollicitat ut habeat. Satis habemus opum, soror, conemur adipisci doctrinam. Vale. Apud St. Germanum, die ultimo anni 1554.

DEBEMUS velle (amica summa sua et soror) dum iuvenes sumus, emmendari ab unoquoque, ut simus citius sapientiores; nec oportet nos dicere modo huic, modo illi: Quid pertinet ad te reprehendere me? Diogenes dicebat Xeniadæ a quo emptus erat, etiam si servus sum, tamen necesse est ut tu mihi pareas, quia qui habet nauclerum, vel medicum servum, cogitur illi obedire, si velit percipere utilitatem ab illo. Non obliviscar tibi dicere modo intellexisse me regem

LIX.

EPENETUS avoit coutume de dire les menteurs estre auteurs de tous crimes et toutes iniures.   Laquelle sentence ne discorde point aus lettres des Hebreus, lesquelles narrent que par la menterie du serpent les portes ont esté ouvertes a tout genre de vice.   Par ce nom de menterie sont aussi contenus les flateurs, calumniateurs, mechans conseilleurs et maulvais gouverneurs, qui sont fontaine de tous maulx.   Puis donc que tant le mensonge deplait a Dieu et [est] si dommageable aus hommes, faisons, ma seur, que touiours soions veritables.

LX.

PLUSIEURS belles histoires temoignent que les anciens ont esté plus studieus de la Rep. et salut des citoiens, que ceus qui ont regné depuis.   Temoin en est Pomponius homme notable et digne de grande louange,

LIX.

M. SC. R. EL. SORORI S. P. D.

EPENETUS dicere solebat mendaces esse autores omnium criminum, et omnium iniuriarum. Quæ senten-
tia non dissonat a literis Hebreorum, quæ narrant ut
mendacio serpentis, fores apertæ fuerunt omni generi
vitiorum. Et hoc nomine mendacium adulatores, ca-
lumniatores, mali consiliarij, et perversi educatores
continentur, qui sunt fontes omnium malorum. Cum
igitur mendacium Deo tantum displiceat, et perniciosum
sit hominibus : faciamus, soror, ut ne quidem ioco
mentiamur, sed simus omne tempore veraces. Vale.
7. Januarij. Apud St. Germanum.

LX.

M. SC. R. EL. SORORI S. P. D.

PLURES pulcræ historiæ testantur veteres fuisse stu-
diossiores reipublicæ et salutis civium quam illos qui
regnaverunt ab eo tempore. Ponponius, homo in-
signis et dignus magna laude, testis est, qui multis

lui demanda si le faisoit penser, il vouloit estre son ami? Si tu veus (repondit Pomponius) estre ami aus Romains, je serai aussi le tien. Vous voiés que sa vie ne lui estoit si chère que l'amitié qui portoit a la republique. A St. Germain, 8. de Janvier.

LXI.

TRES élégamment a chanté le poete qui a dit la liberté ne povoir asses estre achetée. Du quel advis estoit Diogenes, très excellent philosophe, qui repondit a ceus qui louoient le bon heur d'Aristote de quoi il vivoit avec le fils d'un roy: Aristote, dit-il, dinne quand il plaist a Alexandre, Diogenes quand il plaist a Diogenes. Voulant dire riens n'estre heureux si liberté défaut. Apprenons donc les arts et bonnes disciplines, ma seur, par lesquelles plus facilement nous acquerrons vertu, nourrice et mère de liberté, car temoin l'ecriture saincte, quicunque fait peché est serviteur d'iceluy.

amicus esse? Si tu, inquit, fueris amicus Romanis me
etiam amicum habebis. Vides amicitiam qua rem-
publicam prosequebatur maiorem et vita ipsa cariorem.
Vale. 8. Ianuarij.

LXI.

M. SC. R. EL. SORORI S. P. D.

Hoc carmen cecinit eleganter poeta,

Non bene pro toto libertas venditur auro.

Cuius opinionis erat Diogenes philosophus eximius,
qui respondit illis qui laudabant felicitatem Aristotelis
quod viveret cum regis filio: Aristoteles, inquit, prandet
quand[o] placet Alexandro, Diogenes quando placet
Diogeni. Significans nihil esse beatum si libertas
desit. Discamus ergo bonas diciplinas et artes, soror,
per quas facilius parabimus virtutem matrem et neutri-
cem libertatis. Nam, ut sta. Scriptura testatur, qui-
cumque facit peccatum servus est peccati. Vale.
9. Ian.

LXII.

DIOGENES disoit les hommes bons estre les images et simulacres de Dieus, plus tost que les statues d'or, d'argent, ou d'airain : car il est propre aus Dieus de bien faire a tous, et ne nuire a personne. Ce que mieus reluit aus sages et aus bons, qu'aus statues quelques precieuses qu'elles soient. Il disoit encores une autre chose que vous louerés grandement, ascavoir, entre les indigens et miserables n'estre tenu celuy qui s'est acquis de bonnes sciences et de bons amis. Mais que celui estoit malheureusement povre qui n'estoit pourveu de quelque vertu.

LXIII.

[*The French has never been written.*]

DIOGENES dicebat bonos viros esse imagines et simul-
acra deorum, potius quam statuas aureas, argenteas,
vel æreas. Nam proprium est deorum bene facere
omnibus et nocere nemini. Id quod magis elucet in
sapientibus et bonis viris quam in statuis quantisvis
(for quantumvis) preciossissimis. Dicebat etiam aliud
quod maxime laudabis, videlicet inter pauperes et miseros
illum non haberi qui sibi paravit bonas scientias, et
probos amicos. Sed eum esse infeliciter egenum qui
non sit preditus aliqua virtute. Vale.

LEGEBAM hodie apud Ciceronem, soror, non oportere
efferri rebus felicibus et prosperis ; nam, ut dixit Solon,
Crejo nemo ant *(for* ante) obitum felix. Rotat omne
fatum, et si fortuna blanditur nobis hodie, cras mina-
tur. Quomodo accidit Policrati regi Samiorum poten-
tissimo, et usque adeo felici ut ab omnio prælio re-
portarit victoriam. Et tamen evenit quod Oretes,
præfectus Ciri rex Persarum eum superavit et afixit

LXIV.

[The French has never been written.]

[THE END.]

missius geramus.   Dicentes cum Davide rege et pro-
pheta, in manibus tuis sortes meæ, non nobis Domine,
non nobis, sed nomini tuo sanctissimo laus, honor et
gloria sit in secula seculorum.   Amen.   Vale.

QUEMADMODUM non debemus efferi quavis bona fortuna que nobis evenit, ita adversa non debemus despondere animum, nec quoquomodo turbari, veluti
legimus de Socrate, qui nunquam visus est vultu aut
hilari magis aut turbato. Xantippæ (*sic*) testatur, quæ
dixit se semper ipsum vidisse eodem vultu exeuntem
domo et revertentem. Porro si sumus pauperes in hoc
seculo, in hoc sumus similes Deo, et patri nostro, qui
non habuit ubi reclinaret caput suum. Si homines
nos odærint, hoc pollicetur nobis gloriam regna *(for
regina)* celorum.   Vale.

[FINIS.]

MAR 29 1933

MAR 7 1942

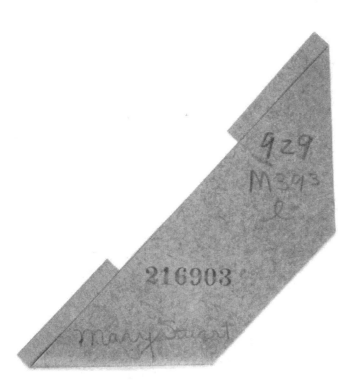

929
M393
e

216903

Mary Saint

51.

12

JOHN DONNE & HIS POETRY

John Donne

JOHN DONNE
& HIS POETRY

BY

F. W. PAYNE M.A. Ph.D.

GEORGE G. HARRAP & CO. LTD.
LONDON   CALCUTTA   SYDNEY

First published 1926
by GEORGE G. HARRAP & CO. LTD.
39–41 Parker Street, Kingsway, London, W.C.2

Printed in Great Britain at THE BALLANTYNE PRESS *by*
SPOTTISWOODE, BALLANTYNE & CO. LTD.
Colchester, London & Eton

GENERAL PREFACE

A GLANCE through the pages of this little book will suffice to disclose the general plan of the series of which it forms a part. Only a few words of explanation, therefore, will be necessary.

The point of departure is the undeniable fact that with the vast majority of young students of literature a living interest in the work of any poet can best be aroused, and an intelligent appreciation of it secured, when it is immediately associated with the character and career of the poet himself. The cases are indeed few and far between in which much fresh light will not be thrown upon a poem by some knowledge of the personality of the writer, while it will often be found that the most direct—perhaps even the only—way to the heart of its meaning lies through a consideration of the circumstances in which it had its birth. The purely æsthetic critic may possibly object that a poem should be regarded simply as a self-contained and detached piece of art, having no personal affiliations or bearings. Of the validity of this as an abstract principle nothing need now be said. The fact remains that, in the earlier stages of study at any rate, poetry is most valued and loved when it is made to seem most human and vital; and the human and vital interest of poetry can be most surely brought home to

5

GENERAL PREFACE

the reader by the biographical method of interpretation.

This is to some extent recognized by writers
of histories and text-books of literature, and by
editors of selections from the works of our
poets ; for place is always given by them to a
certain amount of biographical material. But
in the histories and text-books the biography of
a given writer stands by itself, and his work
has to be sought elsewhere, the student being
left to make the connexion for himself ; while
even in our current editions of selections there
is little systematic attempt to link biography,
step by step, with production.

This brings us at once to the chief purpose
of the present series. In this, biography and
production will be considered together and in
intimate association. In other words, an endeavour will be made to interest the reader in
the lives and personalities of the poets dealt
with, and at the same time to use biography
as an introduction and key to their writings.

Each volume will therefore contain the life-
story of the poet who forms its subject. In this,
attention will be specially directed to his personality as it expressed itself in his poetry, and
to the influences and conditions which counted
most as formative factors in the growth of his
genius. This biographical study will be used
as a setting for a selection, as large as space
will permit, of his representative poems. Such
poems, where possible, will be reproduced in full,

6

GENERAL PREFACE

and care will be taken to bring out their connexion with his character, his circumstances,
and the movement of his mind. Then, in
addition, so much more general literary criticism will be incorporated as may seem to be
needed to supplement the biographical material,
and to exhibit both the essential qualities and
the historical importance of his work.

It is believed that the plan thus pursued is
substantially in the nature of a new departure,
and that the volumes of this series, constituting
as they will an introduction to the study of
some of our greatest poets, will be found useful
to teachers and students of literature, and no
less to the general lover of English poetry.

WILLIAM HENRY HUDSON

ACKNOWLEDGMENT

I AM glad to have the opportunity of thanking Mr S. Rosborough and Mr H. W. Tompkins for their kindness in reading the proofs of this book and for the suggestions they made.

F. W. P.

8

POEMS QUOTED
IN WHOLE

POEMS QUOTED
IN PART

POEMS QUOTED

JOHN DONNE
& HIS POETRY

WE moderns, belonging to a period when men are intensely self-conscious and critical, look back at and, as it seems to us, down on the Middle Ages across a space of three centuries and a half. Gazing, we glimpse an external life almost incredibly picturesque, full of colour and abrupt deeds; but the men of that time, as regards their internal life, their intellectual and spiritual aspirations, appear as though immured in a dark fortress. For in the Middle Ages there was no appeal from authority, which was Holy Church. No man in his right mind doubted that final truth was vested in the Church, and her yoke became hard to bear, for the doctrine she imposed was largely one of repression. She preached continually the divinity of mystical religion, and condemned as evil the body with its primitive instincts, the mind with its independent questionings. Men might, and did, disobey her commands, and indulge the body or the intellect, but, because they believed the Church infallible, it was done in fear and trembling. Therefore the outlook of the age contained large elements of repression and fear. The itch of unsatisfied desires was everywhere, yet terror followed hard upon the steps of licence, whether intellectual or physical. Close on all sides stood the walls of the fortress, holding men back from many forms of self-expression which became for that very reason increasingly desirable.

When the two great classical literatures were rediscovered the appeal of their paganism was irresistible, the walls of the fortress cracked and fell at the shout which arose from within, and Europe rushed out at the breach on the tide of the Renaissance. A vast fund of energy was released, energy which had been accumulating for generations. It was expended recklessly. These men were avid of experience, hungry for knowledge. They plunged into the pursuit of learning; they admired and imitated the classics; they burst into poetry; they experimented eagerly with life from its lowest phases upward. Much of their energy was misdirected, for it must be admitted that at this time zeal was far more prominent than discrimination. Yet in literature this movement produced great things, first in Italy, then in France, finally reaching England as the Elizabethan outburst.

So fine a frenzy could not last long. By the end of the sixteenth century in England these eager tasters of life, hunters of knowledge, worshippers of beauty, were to some extent disillusioned, and knew that some experiences were not worth having, that knowledge can become a burden, that the dazzle of loveliness is liable to blur. This realization produced dissatisfaction, and dissatisfaction is essentially a mood of criticism, which is an appeal to reason.

JOHN DONNE & HIS POETRY

But a literary movement alone could not have initiated a new era in Europe, as this in fact did. Such a dominance implies the support of the whole thought of the time, and the Renaissance reached only a portion of the people, the cultivated classes. They, being more articulate, directed to some extent the thought of the rest, but unless the deepest convictions of the mass had been with them they could not have carried along their age.

In point of fact the Renaissance movement had its counterpart in the world of religion, which was by far the most important department of life. An irreparable breach appeared in the walls of medievalism when in 1517 Luther became the mouthpiece of the tendency we call the Reformation. This was in its beginning, and has been throughout its history, essentially an assertion of reason against authority.

The movement began with the rejection of certain doctrines which it did not seem reasonable to accept, and it expressed a widespread determination of the peoples to think for themselves in matters spiritual as well as temporal.

Therefore the end of the sixteenth century in England presents an arresting spectacle. In the background is a broken medievalism; in the middle distance shows the tide of the Renaissance. But in the foreground wells the spring of an outlook which appeals to reason. Most of the prominent men of this period, though they

13

may have included in their mental and moral make-up something of each of these forces, were dominated by one or the other of them. Bacon, in his plea for experiment in science, embodies the emerging appeal to reason : Spenser is more medieval even than humanist : Sidney is a child of the Renaissance.

But apart from these there stand two figures. One is Shakespeare, here as ever the exception. He is not merely groping toward a rational out-look—he possesses it ; his mind is as startlingly modern as the dress of his thought is unmis-takably of the Renaissance. Yet if Shakespeare, with his great powers and consummate art, stands like a Colossus, towering above his con-temporaries with his eyes fixed in calm certainty on the future, there is another figure nine years farther on, less vast but still a giant, who is Agonistes, the wrestler. For John Donne was the tortured battle-stead of the great forces of his time, and his poetry is the record of the struggle. Any attempt to study Donne's work without a full recognition of this central fact is foredoomed to failure. His early upbringing was medieval and intensely religious. From these early impressions he never shook himself free, deriving from them a deep-rooted ideal of mystical religion, and a tendency to terror-stricken repentance for sin. From the Renais-sance he drew an insatiable desire for knowledge and experience, and this was reinforced by a nature definitely sensuous and sensual. And,

14

finally, he was modern in his critical self-consciousness.

We have noted that many men of Donne's generation combined in themselves these same factors, but in their case one or other of them was permanently in the ascendant. And because in his case these forces were almost equally balanced and perpetually in conflict, Donne is unique. Unique, that is, among those to whom the gods granted self-expression. When art is attacked on utilitarian grounds its upholders are often slow to bring forward one great argument —that it is to art, especially to poetry, that we owe our knowledge of the inner life of ages which are now long past. One real poet gives us more light upon the point of view of a past period than any quantity of dead facts. But it is pathetic to consider how few are those who have the gift of speech. In this first quarter of the seventeenth century which we are discussing there must have been a great number of men who, like Donne, suffered from the impossibility of attaining to unity of outlook; there must have been a few, though very few, in whom the struggle came near to the height of intensity it reached in him; yet to Donne alone was given the power of speech. Therefore he stands to us for his age, and in him we see the interpretation of one phase of it.

Donne never attained to the unity of outlook which he so desired. Even in his last years, when he was living an irreproachable, severely

ascetic life, he found intruding upon his ecstatic
devotion to God faintly alluring remembrances
of former sins, and this cast him into a state of
despair not unmixed with fear.   Time after time
was his serenity destroyed, his poise lost.

And the reason for this is clear.   The modern
principle was not strong enough in him to control
his medieval upbringing.   The highly mystical
form of religion to which he eventually came
was an offspring of his early training; his reason
could never completely master the terror called
up by the 'sins' of his youth.   And Donne's
greatest merit is that he never abandoned the
conflict.   An invincible honesty of endeavour,
rising probably from the depth of his conviction
of the importance of religion, held him back
from the easy solution of accepting, out of sheer
weariness, a faith ready to hand in one of the
churches.   Instead, he worked out his own solution, and spent the latter half of his life in a fierce
endeavour to subdue his body to the ideal which
he had set himself to reach.

In Donne's poetry we find in action the same
factors that we have seen in his character. The
Middle Ages contribute scholastic learning and
a delight in mere logic; also, more important
still—for it is the chief stumbling-block to the
modern reader—the idea that these are fit source
from which to draw the decorative matter for
poetry. The Renaissance quality occurs in the
intense intellectual activity displayed, and in the
purely pagan outlook which is seen in the natur-

alism of the early poems. On the other hand, his innovations both in spirit, metre, and kind give evidence of a new outlook.

Professor Saintsbury says that it is inevitable that many shall not appreciate Donne, less, one gathers, on account of his difficulty than because of the sensual quality of much of his work. This may be so, yet it is difficult to imagine a poet unread in these days for such a reason. Naturalism is indeed beyond the pale, but the average man now has reached a point from which he may well look over without being thought to peep through. However that may be, no one can read Donne with any sincerity and deny him genius. He has the passionate intensity, the imperious need for expression, the leaping imagination which distinguish poets of the first class. What hinders, then, to count him among our greatest?

The impediments are various and serious. In the first place, like Swift, he seemed not to appreciate beauty, if such a thing can be said of one who hated ugliness so intensely. External nature thus had little charm for him; at least, it enters very seldom into his imagery. Whether a sense of the delightfulness of nature is necessary to great art is a separate question; the fact remains that we expect to find it in great poetry. In any case, something must be put in its place, and one is almost tempted to say that Donne has substituted a sense of almost mathematical appropriateness, as though he derived more pleasure from contemplation of a straight line than from gazing at a stretch of green grass. Since it is at least possible that he is right in that choice, although we may differ from him, it behoves us to be careful how we assess this trait. All we can safely say is that it makes his verse less pleasant to read, in our opinion. Another fault Donne had which is certainly of far wider reach, and perhaps more vital. He was not, except instinctively, a literary artist. His work is full of essential artistry, but it is not deliberate. Certainly he had no care to polish his work. The state in which his poems have come down to us sufficiently attests this. Donne's one desire was to discharge his soul of the mood which held him; that done, he probably never turned to his poem again.

The result is that nowhere, except in an occasional short piece, is there the perfect balance which is the culminating merit of a work of art. Again, he seemed lacking in constructive power for a poem on the large scale. The only one he attempted was left unfinished, and the fragment is by no means promising.

These are heavy counts against one who would aspire to the first class among poets, yet Donne's genius will not always be denied. In spite of his indifference to beauty, in spite of the suspect nature of much of his imagery, in spite too of the casuistry with which he loads his verse, his native inspiration at times prevails, and we find here a phrase, there a stanza, now

a complete poem which is, as Professor Saintsbury says in another connexion, poetry *sans
phrase*.

In forming an estimate of the importance of
Donne, to his genius must be added the great
historical significance of his innovations. Not
only did he reject contemptuously the conventional dress of the poetry of his day and substitute
another, but he originated one type of poetry in
England, and changed the spirit of a second. It
is safe to prophesy that as a result of examining
his poetry every reader will be convinced of the
great originality of Donne, that most will admire
the persistent honesty of purpose with which he
maintained his search for truth, that many will
thrill to the genius which places him, though
but occasionally, among those great poets whose
words echo down the imagination, striking out
notes of sympathy on either hand.

II

JOHN DONNE, whose name was variously
spelt, and pronounced to rime with 'done,'
was born in London in 1573, in Bread
Street, being the son of a wealthy ironmonger.
That he was Warden of the Ironmongers'
Company in 1574 is almost the only fact extant
about the poet's father, and the history of the
Donne family is unknown. On the mother's
side, however, there was distinction and to
spare. She was Elizabeth, third daughter of

John Heywood, the celebrated wit and writer of interludes. He lost his position as favourite of Henry VIII by refusing to acknowledge the royal supremacy, and only saved his life by a public recantation. Thereafter, except during Mary's short reign, when he was restored to great favour, he lived in exile at Louvain or Malines. But a greater than John Heywood appears among Donne's ancestors. Heywood's wife, Elizabeth Rastell, was the granddaughter of Elizabeth, sister of Sir Thomas More, the illustrious and ill-fated Chancellor to Henry VIII.

It will be readily understood that the Catholic faith, consecrated by the sacrifice of the life of one ancestor of great renown, and the estates of more than one, became the most cherished possession of Donne's mother; and, it being a curious fact that religious devotion thrives on persecution, her enthusiasm was doubtless strengthened by the troubles that constantly overtook the family, which suffered in every outburst against the Catholics.

We can scarcely doubt, therefore, that Donne was brought up in an intensely religious atmosphere. His father died when the boy was three years old, and it seems probable that he spent some time thereafter with his grandfather, the illustrious John Heywood, at Louvain or Malines. But Heywood died about 1580, and then in all probability John returned to England.

To understand the prominence of religious questions in the early years of our poet it must

be remembered that during that period his
grandfather was deprived of his estates and an
uncle was driven out of his house by a mob. In
1581 another uncle, Father Jasper Heywood,
arrived in England on a mission from Rome, and
was ultimately put into prison, where he languished for some years. Under persecution
such as this, religious belief either breaks down
or is intensified: one can imagine how the
supreme importance of religion was impressed
upon John Donne. It is with great difficulty
that a man, even if he so desires, rids himself of
the teachings of his childhood, and it is important
to note that an element of the outlook which
Donne absorbed in early life remained with him
to the end. Meanwhile, on the secular side the
lad passed for a prodigy. From 1580 to 1583
he had tutors who grounded him in Latin and
French. Some one, possibly the Uncle Jasper
referred to above, likened him to Pico della
Mirandola, who '' was rather born wise than
made so by study.'' In 1584, at the age of
eleven, he was entered at Hart Hall, Oxford,
with his brother Henry, who was a year younger
than himself. It was no uncommon thing for
Catholic children to be sent to the universities
very young, that they might have the benefit
of the course without taking the oaths required
of more mature students. Here Donne stayed
for two years, according to Walton, and then,
without attempting to take a degree, which involved the oath of allegiance, was transferred to

Cambridge. His residence in Oxford is important chiefly because it seems probable that there he first became interested in the study of Spanish thought and literature. There is no doubt that he was unusually well read in the mystics of that nation, and Oxford at this time was a centre of Spanish culture. At Cambridge, where he resided until 1589, "he was," says Walton, "a most laborious student, often changing his studies, but endeavouring to take no degree, for the reasons formerly mentioned." At Cambridge he probably studied mathematics and the sciences.

At the age of seventeen, then, Donne had completed five years of university training, and, having brilliant abilities and a vast desire for knowledge, was regarded as a phenomenon of learning. Throughout all this period Walton says that his tutors "were advised to instil into him particular principles of the Romish Church; of which those tutors professed, though secretly, themselves to be members." The next information we have concerning him, and the first which is attested by documentary evidence, is his entry at Lincoln's Inn in 1592.

The reader has probably been annoyed by the reservations implied above concerning statements by Izaak Walton in his "Life of Dr John Donne," and doubtless argues that since Walton knew Donne his evidence should be accepted. As a matter of fact, Walton knew Donne only during the last and most saintly period of his life; and, exquisite piece of work though his account is, it suffers as a biography because he was concerned to gloss over the earlier portion of Donne's life in order to make it fit in with the highly edifying end, and because his knowledge of the facts of Donne's younger life was inadequate. An example occurs at the point which we have reached.

At some period of his youth Donne travelled extensively in Spain and Italy. Walton says that, having accompanied the Earl of Essex on the Cadiz and Azores expeditions, which took place in 1596 and 1597, Donne " returned not back to England, till he had stayed some years, first in Italy, and then in Spain." Now this is impossible, for during these very years Donne held a promising post in England. What is more probable is that, having completed his university training and come into a share of his father's wealth, Donne followed the custom of the well-to-do youth of his day, and travelled on the Continent. This would account for the two years following 1589, of which no record is extant, and is supported by a portrait of Donne which appears in the 1635 and 1639 editions of his works. It shows him as a youth, and is inscribed *Anno Dni.* 1591. *Ætatis suæ* 18. *Antes muerto que mudado.* The Spanish motto seems rather significant, but nothing certain can be deduced. However he had spent the time since leaving Cambridge, Donne was entered at Lincoln's Inn on May 6, 1592. He had already been a member of Thavies Inn, where his brother Henry had chambers. The latter's career was to be tragically short. In the following year he was arrested for having sheltered a Romish priest, and was thrown into the Clink, where he died of gaol fever, being then nineteen years old.

If the biographer of Donne is lamentably short of facts as material, at least the physical appearance of his subject is well known to him, for there exist no fewer than four portraits of Donne. The first of these is that mentioned above, and before attempting to reconstruct from his poetry the life of this remarkable young man it may be well to see if any aid can be obtained from the portrait, dated one year previously. Certain details of the face are clear enough; we find a large nose coarsely moulded at the base, and thick, full lips. Both of these features are generally understood to indicate a sensual strain in the character. The eyes are large, and look as though they were prominent, and here lies the crux of the face. If those eyes were bold and staring, then the arrogance which is usually spoken of in connexion with the painting might be assumed; but as they may have been clear and keen, or intelligent and sensitive, it is difficult to see how such a deduction can be made. The expression of a face depends so much upon the eyes that an arrogant look can hardly be assumed. Something there is, however, which has probably given rise to the idea, and which is the most striking thing about the portrait—

24

an exceedingly mature look of the face. The portrait looks out at one with the appraising gaze of a man of thirty. The signs of youth are remarkably slight, and chiefly external. Certain contours of the face are inevitably smooth, for after all he was but a lad of eighteen; the Spanish tag in the right-hand top corner corresponds to the forgotten luggage-label of modern days. There remain to be noted the dress, which is more or less military in type, and the grip of the right hand on a sword-hilt. If we are right in supposing that Donne was abroad between 1589 and 1591 it is quite possible that he served in some minor foreign campaign, for he was emphatically of the type that welcomes trouble wherever it may be found. It is more probable that the dress represents merely some fad for simplicity, and that the sword-hilt is simply a claim to rank.

Whether the face was a pleasant one, then, can hardly be determined; it certainly shows signs of a passionate nature. What is certain is that in viewing it one feels the impact of a weight of level, piercing intelligence seldom found in one so young. No one need be surprised if a consciousness of such mental powers resulted in arrogance; the phenomenon is not unknown.

One other thing calls for remark. It follows almost as a corollary to what has been said of the remarkable maturity of this portrait that the face shows no sign of the casual gaiety of youth.

25

Instead there is a distinct suggestion of thoughtful brooding.

Of Donne's life from 1592 until 1596 no actual facts are known, but it is possible to reconstruct the main course of events from the poetry which he wrote during this period.[1]

The sections in which appear the poems written during the years about to be considered are "The Satyres," "Songs and Sonnets," "Elegies," "Epithalamions," and "Letters to Several Personages," but works in these sections may belong to a later date.

We can well believe that Donne, being settled at Lincoln's Inn, possessed of ample means, and with his independence no longer fettered by tutors, turned the vitality which had hitherto made him remarkable as a scholar into observation of the life about him, and after only a few months we find this resulting in verse which indicates at once the youth of the author and his extreme originality. He introduced into English satire of the classical type. Satire was prominent enough in medieval England. Skelton excelled in it, Spenser perhaps gave it its best expression in his description of a suitor's woes, but that of Donne is different. Medieval satire was essentially a torrent of invective against some particular abuse; the classical form is a work of art in which life is deliberately drawn in its ugliest colours, the avowed intention being

[1] This was first done by Sir Edmund Gosse in "The Life and Letters of Dr John Donne."

so to paint folly and vice that they shall repel. It is generally stated that the first poets who attempted this kind of satire in English were Hall and Marston. They were certainly the first to publish their satires. Between 1597 and 1599 Hall was printing his, Marston's appeared in 1598, and the vogue of both met an abrupt end in 1599, when their works were burned by order of the Bishop of London. Both of these men were younger than Donne, and the manuscript of Donne's first three satires is dated 1593, when he was only twenty years old. It follows almost certainly that Donne was the originator in England of this type of verse,[1] and, had he chosen to print, could have claimed precedence of Hall and Marston. The extract given below comes, therefore, from one of his earliest productions.[2]

> Away thou fondling motley humorist,
> Leave mee, and in this standing woodden chest,
> Consorted with these few bookes, let me lye
> In prison, and here be coffin'd, when I dye;
> Here are Gods conduits, grave Divines; and here
> Natures Secretary, the Philosopher;
> And jolly Statesmen, which teach how to tie
> The sinewes of a cities mistique bodie;
> Here gathering Chroniclers, and by them stand
> Giddie fantastique Poëts of each land.

[1] No account here is made of Lodge's satires in "A Fig for Momus" (1595), because the verse is so soft and vague that the essential spirit of the *genre* is absent. Still, these were written in imitation of Horace's satires.

[2] The text in all poems quoted follows exactly early editions. As the problem of Donne's text is very difficult, owing to careless editing and innumerable MSS., in all cases except those indicated in footnotes the actual reading is that chosen by Professor Grierson for his admirable edition.

Shall I leave all this constant company,
And follow headlong, wild uncertaine thee?
First sweare by thy best love in earnest
(If thou which lov'st all, canst love any best)
Thou wilt not leave mee in the middle street,
Though some more spruce companion thou dost
  meet,
Not though a Captaine do come in thy way
Bright parcell gilt, with forty dead mens pay,
Not though a briske perfum'd piert Courtier
Deigne with a nod, thy courtesie to answer.
Nor come a velvet Justice with a long
Great traine of blew coats, twelve, or fourteen strong,
Wilt thou grin or fawne on him, or prepare
A speech to Court his beautious sonne and heire!
For better or worse take mee, or leave mee :
To take, and leave mee is adultery.

  .   .   .   .   .

But since thou like a contrite penitent,
Charitably warn'd of thy sinnes, dost repent
These vanities, and giddinesses, loe
I shut my chamber doore, and come, lets goe.

  .   .   .   .   .

Now we are in the street; He first of all
Improvidently proud, creepes to the wall,
And so imprisoned, and hem'd in by mee
Sells for a little state high [1] libertie;
Yet though he cannot skip forth now to greet
Every fine silken painted foole we meet,
He them to him with amorous smiles allures,
And grins, smacks, shrugs, and such an itch endures,
As prentises, or schoole-boyes which doe know
Of some gay sport abroad, yet dare not goe.

[1] *high*, 1633, Chambers; *his*, 1635-69, manuscripts and Grierson.

28

And as fidlers stop lowest, at highest sound,
So to the most brave, stoops hee nigh'st the ground.

  .   .   .   .   .

Now leaps he upright, Joggs me, and cryes, Do you
  see
Yonder well favoured youth ?   Which ?   Oh, 'tis
  hee
That dances so divinely ; Oh, said I,
Stand still, must you dance here for company ?
Hee droopt, wee went, till one (which did excell
Th' Indians, in drinking his Tobacco well)
Met us; they talk'd; I whispered, let us goe,
'T may be you smell him not, truely I doe;
He heares not mee, but, on the other side
A many-coloured Peacock having spide,
Leaves him and mee; I for my lost sheep stay;
He followes, overtakes, goes on the way,
Saying, him whom I last left, all repute
For his device, in hansoming a sute,
To judge of lace, pinke, panes, print, cut, and
  plight,
Of all the Court, to have the best conceit;
Our dull Comedians want him, let him goe;
But Oh, God strengthen thee, why stopp'st[1] thou so ?

  .   .   .   .   .

At last his Love he in a windowe spies,
And like light dew exhal'd, he flings from mee
Violently ravish'd to his lechery.

The reader who is acquainted with the rhythm and subject-matter of the average Elizabethan poem will notice at once both the content and ruggedness of this verse. As we shall see from the lyrics dealt with later, as, indeed, the

[1] *stop'st*, 1635-54, Chambers ; *stoop'st*, 1633, 1669, Grierson.

JOHN DONNE & HIS POETRY

specimen already given shows in no small measure, Donne was possessed of a highly acute critical faculty. Just as he could see through the glamour of the fashionable London of his day to the follies and vices below, so he perceived that beneath the sugared rhythm of much of the Elizabethan love-poetry there was nothing worth having; that it was mere imitation of the Italian, that the very honey of its phrases was conventional.

Against this the downrightness of Donne's soul revolted, and he went to the opposite extreme. For love-nonsense he would substitute realism; for honey, harshness. The actual form of his revolt was probably influenced by a new movement which had been gaining strength for some time. When Casaubon succeeded Scaliger in the Chair of Greek at the University of Geneva, he drew attention to the claims of Persius as opposed to Juvenal and Horace. Of the three satirists Persius had hitherto been neglected, because he was considered obscure in meaning and harsh in metre. The first of these assumptions Casaubon vigorously denied, but made little reference to the second. The result was that Persius came to pass for the ideal satirist, and, since for most people he remained difficult to read, and no one denied that his verse was irregular, it was assumed by enthusiastic youths like Donne and Hall that some obscurity in meaning and much harshness of metre were an integral part of verse satire. It is almost certain,

30

JOHN DONNE & HIS POETRY

therefore, that those verses in Donne's satire which no method of accenting will cause to scan were deliberate.

This complete break with tradition is proof enough of the extreme independence of Donne, but more evidence is available. In 1593 the five-foot line, whether rimed or free, had to be written true to the norm. It was years later that writers, with Shakespeare in the lead, relaxed the strict laws governing the verse. Yet here we find in Donne's couplets run-on lines, the variable cæsura—in short, a general freedom which recalls Shakespeare's later blank verse. Finally, Donne anticipated the mode of satire which was to be the recognized type. This neither Hall nor Marston did. Each of them has a rather medieval notion of what constitutes satire. Hall for the most part piles up general invective, while Marston indulges in bitter personal attacks. Donne has a totally different method. He uses a walk in company with a Court 'waterfly,' a dissertation upon whose character forms the *pièce de résistance*, as a thread on which to string a number of biting portraits of other members of the species. There is little, if any, mere personal attack, and no hysterical outcries against vice in general; the satire is conveyed by description, and is seasoned at frequent intervals by sly humour. It was precisely this type which was to become the mode after Casaubon, in 1598, published his edition of Theophrastus.

31

JOHN DONNE & HIS POETRY

Enough has been said to show the independence and originality of which Donne gave proof in this his earliest literary venture. As poetry this is not of his best, yet one imagines that any critic reading it as a first attempt would prophesy that here was a writer destined to achievement. The first four lines are excellent; the expression of lines 11 and 12 could scarcely be improved; the description of the captain

> Bright parcell gilt, with forty dead mens pay,

is like a magnesium flash. How could the lines

> As prentises, or schoole-boyes which doe know
> Of some gay sport abroad, yet dare not goe,

be bettered? An excellent humour plays through the whole poem, as in the comment on the man who, in taking the wall,

> Sells for a little state high libertie;

also in the exceedingly fine line, by far the best in the poem,

> And like light dew exhal'd, he flings from mee.

Humorous too, but in a lower grade, is

> 'T may be you smell him not; truely I doe;

while the comic resignation in

> But Oh, God strengthen thee, why stopp'st thou so?

is laughable in the extreme.

But apart from individual beauties, the piece

is interesting. The 'drive' which is a distinguishing mark of all Donne's poetry is fully in evidence, and when it is remembered that the roughnesses of metre are largely deliberate it can be safely affirmed that not many young men of twenty-one could present so promising a copy of verses.

Of the writer's character the satire seems to give a most illuminating glimpse. We see so clearly the young man, for the first time, perhaps, free from parental and tutorial control, settled in his rooms, and examining with eager interest the life about him. His pose of the reluctant student is a pleasant subterfuge. He takes little persuading, "and come, lets goe." In reality he is all agog to experience this new world. His sense of humour, too, is a thing pleasant to see, for in future it will be frequently embittered. Under the influence of passion its mordancy will develop too readily into cruelty. For the present he is merely observing and tasting, adventuring abroad and then retreating to his study to record his impressions with clear-sighted humour and the unconscious insolence of youth.

Presently his lyrics will show us some of his adventures, but before that we see yet another side of the character of this rather protean youth, and in the process obtain our last glimpse of his satires.

An objection which can be brought against the one already considered is that it is too trivial.

JOHN DONNE & HIS POETRY

Satire needs gravity of purpose to justify it and
to give dignity to its exposures. Whatever else
it lacks the third satire of Donne has this qualification, for in it he sets out at length his attitude
toward religion, upbraids himself for neglect
of it, and enjoins upon himself and others a
strenuous search for truth. It was probably at
this time, not two years earlier, as Walton says,
that Donne "began seriously to survey and consider the body of divinity, as it was then con-
troverted betwixt the reformed and the Roman
Church. . . . Being to undertake this search,
he believed the Cardinal Bellarmine to be the
best defender of the Roman Cause, and therefore
betook himself to the examination of his reasons
. . . and about the twentieth year of his age did
show the then Dean of Gloucester . . . all the
Cardinal's works marked with many weighty
observations under his own hand."

Stress has already been laid upon the urgency
with which the importance of religious faith
was laid upon Donne in his youth ; it says
much for the permanency of the effect that
here, in the full tide of his youth, amid a crowd
of other and exceedingly mundane pursuits, he
should be meditating, with a sincerity which the
reader will certainly recognize, the means of
attaining to a settled faith. It was almost inevitable, considering his mode of life, his insatiable intellectual curiosity, and his range of
reading, that Donne should have drifted far from
his childish beliefs. Almost every intelligent

34

youth does that, and Donne's critical faculty was so prominent that the process in his case was probably both early and very complete. Yet this satire makes it clear that he was at bottom aware of the necessity for him of a faith. The need has not yet become urgent. There is here little sign of emotional disturbance, his approach to the question being rather intellectual; he is none the less in earnest.

After a few introductory lines he begins:

Is not our Mistresse faire Religion,
As worthy of all our Soules devotion,
As vertue was to the first blinded age?
Are not heavens joyes as valiant to asswage
Lusts, as earths honour was to them?   Alas,
As wee do them in meanes, shall they surpasse
Us in the end, and shall thy fathers spirit
Meete blinde Philosophers in heaven, whose merit
Of strict life may be imputed faith, and heare
Thee, whom hee taught so easie wayes and neare
To follow, damn'd?   O if thou dar'st, feare this;
This feare great courage, and high valour is.

There follow examples of desperate courage exercised for gain, or to satisfy a point of honour; the soul is reproached for neglecting God's war against " the foul devil " in order to prosecute these other ventures; then comes the exhortation.

Seeke true religion.   O where?   Mirreus
Thinking her unhous'd here, and fled from us,
Seekes her at Rome; there, because hee doth
      know
That shee was there a thousand yeares agoe,

He loves her ragges so, as wee here obey
The statecloth where the Prince sate yesterday.
Crantz to such brave Loves will not be inthrall'd,
But loves her onely, who at Geneva is call'd
Religion, plaine, simple, sullen, yong,
Contemptuous, yet unhansome.

This gibe at the expense of Rome indicates
that Donne is by no means disposed to accept
Papal authority, while the very appropriate
description of the Calvinistic doctrine, then comparatively ' young,' shows how its harsh exclu-
siveness repels him. The Church of England was
evidently too artificial a compromise to suit his
mood.

Graius stayes still at home here, and because
Some Preachers, vile ambitious bauds, and lawes
Still new like fashions, bid him thinke that shee
Which dwels with us, is onely perfect, hee
Imbraceth her, whom his Godfathers will
Tender to him, being tender, as Wards still
Take such wives as their Guardians offer, or
Pay valewes.

After describing an indifferent man,

Carelesse Phrygius doth abhorre
All, because all cannot be good,

and a man uncritical of creeds,

Gracchus loves all as one, and thinks that so
As women do in divers countries goe
In divers habits, yet are still one kinde,
So doth, so is Religion ; and this blind-
nesse too much light breeds,

JOHN DONNE & HIS POETRY

Donne states his own position and attitude in a passage which, at any rate in parts, deserves the epithet noble.

> But unmoved thou
> Of force must one, and forc'd but one allow ;
> And the right ; aske thy father which is shee,
> Let him aske his ; though truth and falshood bee
> Neare twins, yet truth a little elder is ;
> Be busie to seeke her, beleeve mee this,
> Hee's not of none, nor worst, that seekes the best.
> To adore, or scorne an image, or protest,
> May all be bad ; doubt wisely ; in strange way
> To stand inquiring right, is not to stray ;
> To sleepe, or runne wrong, is. On a huge hill,
> Cragged, and steep, Truth stands, and hee that will
> Reach her, about must, and about must goe ;
> And what the hills suddennes resists, winne so ;
> Yet strive so, that before age, deaths twilight,
> Thy Soule rest, for none can worke in that night.
> To will, implyes delay, therefore now doe :
> Hard deeds, the bodies paines ; hard knowledge too
> The mindes indeavours reach, and mysteries
> Are like the Sunne, dazling, yet plaine to all eyes.
> Keepe the truth which thou hast found ; men do
>   not stand
> In so ill case here, that God hath with his hand
> Sign'd Kings blanck-charters to kill whom they
>   hate,
> ‹ Nor are they Vicars, but hangmen to Fate.
> Foole and wretch, wilt thou let thy Soule be tyed
> To mans lawes, by which she shall not be tryed
> At the last day ? Oh, will it then boot thee
> To say a Philip, or a Gregory,
> A Harry, or a Martin taught thee this?

Is not this excuse for mere contraries,
Equally strong ? cannot both sides say so ?
That thou mayest rightly obey power, her bounds
 know ;
Those past, her nature, and name is chang'd; to be
Then humble to her is idolatrie.

The first sixteen lines of this extract combine
dignity and strength, the latter rather enhanced
than lessened by the metrical abruptness.   The
man who writes

 Beleeve mee this,
 Hee's not of none, nor worst, that seekes the best

cannot be set aside as a trifler. From the beginning of the passage can be felt the tension of
emotion, which was the one thing that would
free from trammels Donne's power of expression.
Accordingly, here at the climax he gives us in
the description of Truth one of those bright
flashes of pure poetry with which he rewards
those who pursue him.

 On a huge hill,
 Cragged, and steep, Truth stands.

III

IT was noted earlier in this book that the
most striking feature of Donne's life was
the constant warring of the diverse elements
of his character. We have just seen him resolv-
ing, with a sincerity which cannot be doubted,
upon a search for spiritual truth; a while ago
he was stripping the life about him of its

shams and seeing it as it was, not as it would fain appear. Both of these attempts were, at least in part, the outcome of an intense curiosity, though it is true that behind the former lay something else which was later to become prominent. This overwhelming desire for knowledge and experience of every kind was typical of the Renaissance, and Donne with his great vitality was not likely to stand entirely aloof from the opportunities for amorous adventure which would come to him from every side. And in considering his attitude to this aspect of life it must be remembered that the pagan element was peculiarly strong in these Renaissance men, of whom probably none had such a store of eager energy as distinguished Donne. The fact cannot be put aside, although attempts at doing so have not been lacking, that the highly sensual poetry which Donne produced at this period of his life was based upon actual experience. No one can read it with any care and doubt this, for there is present in much of it a most convincing sincerity. But the picture must not be too heavily coloured. Amorous adventure, although naturally it was the focusing-point of his power of expression, formed but a small part of Donne's life. We have already seen him as a curious observer of manners and as an intellectual searcher after truth. In addition he studied law with voracity. Walton expressly notes the fact: "he gave great testimonies of his wit, his learning, and of his improvement in that profession." In after years it was said of Donne that he "knew all laws," and Walton states that at a later date "he acquired [in law] such a perfection, as was judged to hold proportion with many who had made that study the employment of their whole life."

Of Donne's life for the next three years no single detail is actually known. Whether or not he travelled, his success as a student, the exact circle in which he moved—all is obscurity, except that we know that he was acquainted with Ben Jonson, and that certain of his friends, who will be mentioned later, were extremely well connected. Did Donne frequent the Mermaid Tavern? Did he know Shakespeare? These are questions which spring at once to the mind, but to which there is at present no answer.

Our only source of information is a body of undated and unarranged poetry, dealing with one phase only of his life. After long and careful consideration of the "Songs and Sonnets" (that is to say, 'lyrics,' for there is not one formal sonnet among them) and "The Elegies," Sir Edmund Gosse came to the conclusion that certain episodes can be clearly traced in them. The only alternative to this conclusion is that Donne wrote a series of love-poems based on an imaginary intrigue. To the mind of the present writer this almost proves the original proposition, for the violence of personal passion in the poems makes the second unthinkable. Moreover, oblique art of this kind was not in Donne's nature; he was nothing if not direct.

In these poems we see Donne first in the full tide of his eagerness, flitting here and there, taking love lightly wherever it could be found. The following virile outburst shows him exulting in his new emotions.

THE GOOD-MORROW

I wonder by my troth, what thou, and I
Did, till we lov'd ? were we not wean'd till then?
But suck'd on countrey pleasures, childishly?
Or snorted we in the seaven sleepers den?
T'was so ; But this, all pleasures fancies bee.
If ever any beauty I did see,
Which I desir'd, and got, t'was but a dreame of
    thee.

And now good morrow to our waking soules,
Which watch not one another out of feare ;
For love, all love of other sights controules,
And makes one little roome, an every where.
Let sea-discoverers to new worlds have gone,
Let Maps to other, worlds on worlds have showne,
Let us possesse one world, each hath one, and is
    one.

My face in thine eye, thine in mine appeares,
And true plaine hearts doe in the faces rest,
Where can we finde two better hemispheares ·
Without sharpe North, without declining West?
What ever dyes, was not mixt equally ;
If our two loves be one, or, thou and I
Love so alike, that none doe slacken, none can
    die.

JOHN DONNE & HIS POETRY

In this little poem we have the adult manner of Donne. Practically every element is present. The first line and a half gives one of those magical phrases which lift his verse out of the common rut. Throughout the piece we feel the directness of impact which is the outstanding characteristic of his phrasing. In stanzas two and three we find the type of imagery which most distinguished him from his contemporaries. Temperamentally averse to the sweetness and artificiality of the love-poetry of his time, he attempts realism, as has been already seen in his satires. Tired of the worn-out conventions of classical imagery he turns to the contemporary life in which he had such vivid interest. One of the chief preoccupations of his time was geographical discoveries, which accordingly are pressed into service.

It has already been said that he seemed to lack a sense of beauty, for which he substitutes mathematical appropriateness. The result is that as long as his comparison is accurate, and has point, he does not perceive that frequently it is grotesque. And here a word of warning may be in season. To modern taste natural imagery may be more suitable to poetry than the geographical sort, but there is no absolute criterion in these matters. Let those of us at any rate who cannot for our lives attain to Donne's poetic capacity regard it as at least possible that his judgment may be correct, remembering how the early pre-Raphaelite pictures of Millais

JOHN DONNE & HIS POETRY

were abused by the "Times" as heartily as Epstein's Hudson memorial, and on identical grounds—namely, that they were appallingly ugly.

But whether or no they are beautiful, Donne's figures are meticulously accurate, and to get into sympathy with him they must be carefully studied. This poem affords an example. In line 17 appears the word 'hemispheares.' A casual reader would say that by these Donne meant either 'faces' or 'parts.' Actually he means that each lover's face is a world to the other, and the point lies in the fact that in a reflection of a globe only half can appear. The next line contains two epithets of exquisite justness. Another constant trait of Donne, occasional obscurity, is also found here, for it needs careful reading to make line 13 yield up its sense. Yet a reader who refuses to make any allowances will still be impressed by the poem. The impetus of the author carries one along, while the first stanza is very good indeed.

Another mood of these early days, this time a gay and boisterous one, is expressed in "The Sunne Rising," of which the first stanza is given here.

> Busie old foole, unruly Sunne,
> Why dost thou thus,
> Through windowes, and through curtaines call on
> us?
> Must to thy motions lovers seasons run?
> Sawcy pedantique wretch, goe chide
> Late schoole boyes, and sowre prentices,

43

> Goe tell Court-huntsmen, that the King will
>   ride,
> Call countrey ants to harvest offices;
> Love, all alike, no season knowes, nor clyme,
> Nor houres, dayes, moneths, which are the rags
>   of time.

This is the *aubade* metamorphosed with a vengeance. Compare it with that in *Romeo and Juliet*, probably written about the same time. In its way this is a splendid thing. It has a very complete unity, of a mood so masculine and exultant that the verse positively tramples in expressing it.

In another piece we find him rejoicing openly in aggressive liberty. Not for him one love and the ties of affection, but many loves and freedom. Certainly in the last two lines of the first stanza the strong man rejoices in his youth.

THE INDIFFERENT

> I can love both faire and browne,
> Her whom abundance melts, and her whom want
>   betraies,
> Her who loves lonenesse best, and her who maskes
>   and plaies,
> Her whom the country form'd, and whom the town,
> Her who beleeves, and her who tries,
> Her who still weepes with spungie eyes,
> And her who is dry corke, and never cries;
> I can love her, and her, and you and you,
> I can love any, so she be not true.
>
> Will no other vice content you?
> Will it not serve your turn to do, as did your
>   mothers?

44

Or have you all old vices spent, and now would
    finde out others?
Or doth a feare, that men are true, torment
    you?
Oh we are not, be not you so,
Let mee, and doe you, twenty know.
Rob mee, but binde me not, and let me goe.
Must I, who came to travaile thorow you,
Grow your fixt subject, because you are true?

Venus heard me sigh this song,
And by Loves sweetest Part, Variety, she swore,
She heard not this till now; and that it should be
    so no more.
She went, examin'd, and return'd ere long,
And said, alas, Some two or three
Poore Heretiques in love there bee,
Which thinke to stablish dangerous constancie.
But I have told them, since you will be true,
You shall be true to them, who are false to you.

It will be observed that in each of the three
poems which have been quoted the first stanza
is much better than the following ones. In
these latter the writer holds the attention by the
force he pours into the line, but the former is
always felicitous to a high degree. The song
given below differs because its parts are equal in
power. So good are all three stanzas that it is
impossible to choose between them. Also in
this, one of his happiest moments, the poet has
attained a strange intangible beauty. Here we
have a merry and subtly varied rhythm (the
reader must be careful to make the stress on

JOHN DONNE & HIS POETRY

'strange' in line 10 and on 'were' in line 23),
exquisite propriety of diction, an absence of far-
fetched imagery, and a most individual use of
the more ordinary sources. The piece, in fact,
gives that effect of simplicity and appropriateness which is termed classical, and ranks with
the best of Dryden's songs, than which few
indeed are better.

SONG: GOE, AND CATCHE A FALLING
STARRE

Goe, and catche a falling starre,
    Get with child a mandrake roote,
Tell me, where all past yeares are,
    Or who cleft the Divels foot,
Teach me to heare Mermaides singing,
    Or to keep off envies stinging,
            And finde
            What winde
Serves to advance an honest minde.

If thou beest borne to strange sights,
    Things invisible to see,
Ride ten thousand daies and nights,
    Till age snow white haires on thee,
Thou, when thou retorn'st, wilt tell mee
    All strange wonders that befell thee,
            And sweare
            No where
Lives a woman true, and faire.

If thou findst one, let mee know,
    Such a Pilgrimage were sweet;
Yet doe not, I would not goe,
    Though at next doore wee might meet,

46

JOHN DONNE & HIS POETRY

> Though shee were true, when you met her,
> And last, till you write your letter,
>> Yet shee
>> Will bee
> False, ere I come, to two, or three.

This lighthearted gibe at women cloaks no
heartache. It is obviously an expression of the
cynicism of youth, that time-honoured excuse
for the outpouring of cleverness. Nevertheless,
this phase of amorous buccaneering could not,
in the nature of things, endure. One of two
things was bound to happen. Either the subject
would tire of the game or he would be entangled
by a genuine passion. Donne's fate was the
latter. The history of this affair is given for the
most part (though not entirely) among "The
Elegies," and probably the fact was recognized
when the name was given to the group of
poems, for they could not possibly be called
elegies in the usual sense of the term—that
is, lament. They are elegies, however, in the
strict Latin meaning of a series of poems in
which a love-affair is related. Among the
Elizabethans this function was generally rele-
gated to sonnet series, and frequently the love-
motif is purely apocryphal. But if Donne's
poems do not relate a real experience, then he
was an artist far greater than has yet been
suspected.

It is possible that the following verses record
the beginning of Donne's entanglement. At
any rate they are worth quoting, because they

47

JOHN DONNE & HIS POETRY

contain one of the witty conceits for which he
became so famous.

THE BROKEN HEART

He is starke mad, who ever sayes,
   That he hath beene in love an houre,
Yet not that love so soone decayes,
   But that it can tenne in lesse space devour ;
Who will beleeve mee, if I sweare
That I have had the plague a yeare ?
    Who would not laugh at mee, if I should say,
    I saw a flask of *powder burne a day?*

Ah, what a trifle is a heart,
   If once into loves hands it come !
All other griefes allow a part
   To other griefes, and aske themselves but some ;
They come to us, but us Love draws,
Hee swallows us, and never chawes :
   By him, as by chain'd shot, whole rankes doe
     dye,
   He is the tyran Pike, our hearts the Frye.

If 'twere not so, what did become
   Of my heart, when I first saw thee ?
I brought a heart into the roome,
   But from the roome, I carried none with mee :
If it had gone to thee, I know
Mine would have taught thine heart to show
   More pitty unto mee : but Love, alas,
   At one first blow did shiver it as glasse.

Yet nothing can to nothing fall,
   Nor any place be empty quite,
Therefore I thinke my breast hath all
   Those peeces still, though they be not unite ;

48

> And now as broken glasses show
> A hundred lesser faces, so
>> My ragges of heart can like, wish, and adore,
>> But after one such love, can love no more.

In this poem it seems to me we have the whole of Donne as a writer. To take the worst first,

> Hee swallows us, and never chawes,

and

> He is the tyran Pike, our hearts the Frye,

strike one as grotesque, and although this is partly because we only know 'chawes' as a dialect term, and 'frye' as connoting other things, nevertheless the comparisons are in bad taste and crude. Yet they make vivid the meaning. This was the supreme virtue for Donne, for he was bent on realism, intent always to express his intellectual processes in concrete images drawn from actual life, not from an outworn convention. The conceit of the shivered glass is better because it contains nothing disconcerting and is equally apt. As always, Donne has here his offering for the lover of good expression. Who would undertake to improve

> Who would not laugh at mee, if I should say,
> I saw a flask of *powder burne a day?*

Our poet, then, has lost his heart. Gone are the days when he says in " Variety ":

The heavens rejoice in motion, why should I
Abjure my so much lov'd variety,
And not with many youth and love divide?
Pleasure is none, if not diversifi'd:
The sun that sitting in the chaire of light
Sheds flame into what else so ever doth seem
 bright,
Is not contented at one Signe to Inne,
But ends his year and with a new beginnes.
All things doe willingly in change delight,
The fruitfull mother of our appetite:
Rivers the clearer and more pleasing are,
Where their fair spreading streames run wide
 and farr;
And a dead lake that no strange bark doth greet,
Corrupts it self and what doth live in it.
Let no man tell me such a one is faire,
And worthy all alone my love to share.
Nature in her hath done the liberall part
Of a kinde Mistresse, and imploy'd her art
To make her loveable, and I aver
Him not humane that would turn back from
 her:
I love her well, and would, if need were, dye
To doe her service.   But followes it that I
Must serve her onely, when I may have choice
Of other beauties, and in change rejoice?

This *liaison*, as revealed in " The Elegies,"
was a sordid affair.   The lady was married, and
her husband was an invalid who could not stand
or walk, but who maintained a considerable
establishment.   The intrigue was carried on in
his own house, with Donne in the *rôle of visitor*.
This is no place to discuss whether the guilt of

such an affair is really aggravated by conducting it in the house and presence of the injured person, or whether the good taste which dictates a more remote scene of operations is not indeed a sham. It may be safely assumed that to Donne the question never occurred. Capable at any time of almost fierce absorption in a subject, in love he would be heedless of every consideration. Unquestionably at first he enjoyed himself, delighting in the secret assignations, the language of flowers and signs. We can imagine the three at table, the invalid husband, Donne, and the lady; Donne pouring out with secret delight brilliant conversation of which every other sentence contained an ingenious double meaning. It is amusing to imagine the affected language of this conversation with the lady. At first it appears she was something unfashionable of speech, or not too intelligent. Donne taught her to euphuize. She discovered an unsuspected aptitude for intrigue, and evidently showed signs at one time of extending the scope of her operations, for we find Donne in a violently jealous mood.

ELEGIE VII : NATURES LAY IDEOT

Natures lay Ideot, I taught thee to love,
And in that sophistrie, Oh, thou dost prove
Too subtile: Foole, thou didst not understand
The mystique language of the eye nor hand:
Nor couldst thou judge the difference of the aire
Of sighes, and say, this lies, this sounds despaire:

51

Nor by the eyes water call a maladie
Desperately hot, or changing feaverously.
I had not taught thee then, the Alphabet
Of flowers, how they devisefully being set
And bound up, might with speechlesse secrecie
Deliver arrands mutely, and mutually.
Remember since all thy words us'd to bee
To every suitor; *I, if my friends agree;*
Since, household charmes, thy husbands name to
    teach,
Were all the love trickes, that thy wit could
    reach ;
And since, an houres discourse could scarce have
    made
One answer in thee, and that ill arraid
In broken proverbs, and torne sentences.
Thou art not by so many duties his,
That from the worlds Common having sever'd
    thee,
Inlaid thee, neither to be seene, nor see,
As mine: who have with amorous delicacies
Refin'd thee into a blis-ful Paradise.
Thy graces and good words my creatures bee ;
I planted knowledge and lifes tree in thee,
Which Oh, shall strangers taste ?   Must I alas
Frame and enamell Plate, and drinke in Glasse ?
Chafe waxe for others seales ? breake a colts
    force
And leave him then, beeing made a ready horse ?

Evidently Donne took a keen pleasure in practising the elaborate art of love affected at that time. The next quotation—from "Elegie I: Jealosie"—shows the ugly side of the affair, and Donne's strange indifference to it.

Fond woman, which would'st have thy husband
    die,
And yet complain'st of his great jealousie;
If swolne with poyson, hee lay in his last bed,
His body with a sere-barke covered,

.   .   .   .   .

Thou would'st not weepé, but jolly, and frolicke
    bee,
As a slave, which to morrow should be free;
Yet weep'st thou, when thou seest him hungerly
Swallow his owne death, hearts-bane jealousie.
O give him many thanks, he is courteous,
That in suspecting kindly warneth us.
Wee must not, as wee us'd, flout openly,
In scoffing ridles, his deformitie;
Nor at his boord together being satt,
With words, nor touch, scarce lookes adulterate.
Nor when he swolne, and pamper'd with great fare,
Sits downe, and snorts, cag'd in his basket chaire,
Must wee usurpe his owne bed any more,
Nor kisse and play in his house, as before.
Now I see many dangers; for that is
His realme, his castle, and his diocesse.
But if, as envious men, which would revile
Their Prince, or coyne his gold, themselves exile
Into another countrie, and doe it there,
Wee play in another house, what should we feare?
There we will scorne his houshold policies,
His seely plots, and pensionary spies,
As the inhabitants of Thames right side
Do Londons Major; or Germans, the Popes pride.

It is clear that now the love-making has been in progress for a long time, and that the husband's suspicions are aroused. Also it would appear

JOHN DONNE & HIS POETRY

that Donne is no longer in the earliest stage of adoration.

It is probable that this poem brings us to the beginning of the year 1596, during which Donne went with the expedition to Cadiz, which will be discussed later. In 1597 he went with Essex to the Azores, and in a verse letter to a friend[1] suggests that one of the reasons for his going on the expedition was

> . . . to disuse mee from the queasie paine
> Of being belov'd, and loving.

Is it not likely, therefore, that he kept his resolution to be discreet by volunteering for foreign service? Certainly before he went he sent the lady his picture, accompanying it by a poem in which the most is made of the destructive possibilities of campaigning.

ELEGIE V: HIS PICTURE

Here take my Picture; though I bid farewell,
Thine, in my heart, where my soule dwels, shall
　　dwell.
'Tis like me now, but I dead, 'twill be more
When wee are shadowes both, then 'twas before.
When weather-beaten I come backe; my hand,
Perhaps with rude oares torne, or Sun beams
　　tann'd,
My face and brest of hairecloth, and my head
With cares rash sodaine stormes, being o'rspread,
My body a sack of bones, broken within,
And powders blew staines scatter'd on my skinne;

[1] See pages 66–67.

54

> If rivall fooles taxe thee to have lov'd a man,
> So foule, and course, as, Oh, I may seeme than,
> This shall say what I was: and thou shalt say,
> Doe his hurts reach mee ? doth my worth decay ?
> Or doe they reach his judging minde, that hee
> Should now love lesse, what hee did love to see ?
> That which in him was faire and delicate,
> Was but the milke, which in loves childish state
> Did nurse it : who now is growne strong enough
> To feed on that, which to disused tasts seemes
>   tough.

The chances are that during Donne's absence in 1596 and 1597 the *liaison* died a natural death. Possibly both parties-had recovered to some extent from their infatuation; perhaps the lady had developed wisdom; certainly, after his return, Donne, who was taking up a responsible position, had reasons for wishing to end so compromising an affair.   At any rate such a decision was taken.   In " Elegie XII : His Parting from Her " we see that some real affection had underlain Donne's arrogant love-making.   He begins :

> Since she must go, and I must mourn, come
>   Night,
> Environ me with darkness, whilst I write :
> Shadow that hell unto me, which alone
> I am to suffer when my Love is gone.

Later, in apostrophizing Love, he continues :

> Was't not enough that thou didst dart thy fires
> Into our blouds, inflaming our desires,

And made'st us sigh and glow, and pant, and
    burn,
And then thy self into our flame did'st turn?
Was't not enough, that thou didst hazard us
To paths in love so dark, so dangerous:
And those so ambush'd round with houshold
    spies,
And over all, thy husbands towring eyes
That flam'd with oylie sweat of jealousie:
Yet went we not still on with Constancie?
Have we not kept our guards, like spie on spie?
Had correspondence whilst the foe stood by?
Stoln (more to sweeten them) our many blisses
Of meetings, conference, embracements, kisses?
Shadow'd with negligence our most respects?
Varied our language through all dialects,
Of becks, winks, looks, and often under-boards
Spoak dialogues with our feet far from our words?
Have we prov'd all these secrets of our Art,
Yea, thy pale inwards, and thy panting heart?
And, after all this passed Purgatory,
Must sad divorce make us the vulgar story?

Toward the end of the elegy are found the
most pleasant lines that Donne wrote in this
connexion. Still addressing Love, he says

Do thy great worst, my friend and I have armes,
Though not against thy strokes, against thy harmes.
Rend us in sunder, thou canst not divide
Our bodies so, but that our souls are ty'd,
And we can love by letters still and gifts,
And thoughts and dreams; Love never wanteth
    shifts.
I will not look upon the quickning Sun,
But straight her beauty to my sense shall run;

The ayre shall note her soft, the fire most pure;
Water suggest her clear, and the earth sure.
Time shall not lose our passages; the Spring
How fresh our love was in the beginning;
The Summer how it ripened in the eare;
And Autumn, what our golden harvests were.
The Winter I'll not think on to spite thee,
But count it a lost season, so shall shee.

The couplet

I will not look upon the quickning Sun,
But straight her beauty to my sense shall run,

is excellent, and from there to the end of the quotation the standard is high.

It was not likely, however, that Donne would end the affair on so gentle a note. He was now some years older than when it began, and had high hopes of a career. Calm afterthought threw into relief aspects of the intrigue which pricked his conscience, now beginning to re-assert its sway after the pagan fit; above all, the ignominy of it lashed his pride. It was brooding upon all this which probably gave rise to such pieces as the following, which occurs in the poem called "The Curse."

Who ever guesses, thinks, or dreames he knowes
Who is my mistris, wither by this curse;

.　　　.　　　.　　　.　　　.

The venom of all stepdames, gamsters gall,
What Tyrans, and their subjects interwish,
　　　What Plants, Mynes, Beasts, Foule, Fish,
　　　Can contribute, all ill which all
Prophets, or Poets spake; And all which shall

.　57

Be annex'd in schedules unto this by mee,
Fall on that man; For if it be a shee
Nature before hand hath out-cursed mee.

This, of course, is a mere general outburst, but in the end Donne reached such a pitch of fury that he turned, most unjustly, upon the lady in one of the finest hate poems in the language. There is a cold malignity about it which almost makes one shudder, but the expression is perfect.

THE APPARITION

When by thy scorne, O murdresse, I am dead,
    And that thou thinkst thee free
From all solicitation from mee,
Then shall my ghost come to thy bed,
And thee, fain'd vestall, in worse armes shall see;
Then thy sicke taper will begin to winke,
And he, whose thou art then, being tyr'd before,
Will, if thou stirre, or pinch to wake him, thinke
    Thou call'st for more,
And in false sleepe will from thee shrinke,
And then poore Aspen wretch, neglected thou
Bath'd in a cold quicksilver sweat wilt lye
    A veryer ghost then I;
What I will say, I will not tell thee now,
Lest that preserve thee; and since my love is
    spent,
I had rather thou shouldst painfully repent,
Then by my threatnings rest still innocent.

The reader had already been made aware that the above sequence of events is conjectural. It is safe to assume that it is in the main correct, provided that the poems are based on actual experience, which is made probable by the fact that there are in the collection poems—unquotable here—which prove that Donne had such experience. To me the poems themselves are evidence that they record real incidents. They contain things that surely would not find their way into a poem of pure invention. But if the reader chooses to consider that Donne, standing apart from this side of life, invented these poems from the materials supplied by conversation and a very occasional experience, then he is making a new claim. In any case these lyrics and "The Satyres" show Donne as the first of the great seventeenth-century realists; this view would claim for him powers of dramatic imagination of a high order.

If, then, these poems record for the most part actual facts the question will be asked whether this writer was not a very depraved young man. Viewed in the light of his after career the answer is in the negative. His outstanding characteristic is uncompromising intellectual honesty. He had hidden away a high ideal of conduct, which for the time was overcome by the demands of his exceedingly vigorous body. But he was honest with himself. Many other young men of his time were equally at fault in conduct, but their graceful and conventional love-poems were a sham. Shams of all kind were hateful to Donne, and he revolted from convention to realism. Like most people who head a new movement, he went too far, and his realism is at times crude.

IV

LITTLE is known of Donne's relations with the literary men of the time during these early years of his manhood. Probably he extended dislike of the style of their verse to their persons. The only poet of distinction with whom we know him to have been on cordial terms is Ben Jonson, though there is nothing to show that they were personal friends. Donne wrote to Jonson a copy of Latin verses, and himself won the difficult praises of the dramatist. Several of the latter's comments on Donne are recorded by Drummond of Hawthornden in the notes which he made of his conversations with Jonson, who visited him in the course of a tramp to Scotland. Jonson declared " that Donne, for not keeping of accent deserved hanging," also that he, " for not being understood, would perish." Another dictum recorded by Drummond is that " he esteemeth John Donne the first poet in the world in some things : his verses of ' The Lost Chain ' he hath by heart." Now this is curious, for the piece in question—"Elegie XI : The Bracelet "—is the last of Donne's poems which the modern critic would praise. Nearly half a hundred verses of it are nothing but a toying—ingenious,

but in this bulk unspeakably tedious—with the
two meanings of 'angel' which, besides 'spirit,'
meant also a coin. Shakespeare makes quite
sufficient play with this ancient pun, but Donne
carries it beyond all endurance. He has lost
his mistress's chain, which he regrets, not for
sentimental reasons nor the bad luck it may
bring,

but the bitter cost.

O, shall twelve righteous Angels, which as yet
No leaven of vile soder did admit;
Nor yet by any way have straid or gone
From the first state of their Creation;
Angels, which heaven commanded to provide
All things to me, and be my faithfull guide;
To gaine new friends, t'appease great enemies;
To comfort my soule, when I lie or rise;
Shall these twelve innocents, by thy severe
Sentence (dread judge) my sins great burden beare?
Shall they be damn'd, and in the furnace throwne,
And punisht for offences not their owne?
They save not me, they doe not ease my paines,
When in that hell they are burnt and tyed in
   chains.

After a digression into Continental coinage he
returns to the theme with:

Thou say'st (alas) the gold doth still remaine,
Though it be chang'd, and put into a chaine;
So in the first falne angels, resteth still
Wisdome and knowledge; but, 'tis turn'd to ill:
As these should doe good works; and should
   provide
Necessities; but now must nurse thy pride.

And they are still bad angels; Mine are none;
For, forme gives being, and their forme is gone:
Pitty these Angels; yet their dignities
Passe Vertues, Powers, and Principalities.
    But, thou art resolute; Thy will be done!
Yet with such anguish, as her onely sonne
The Mother in the hungry grave doth lay,
Unto the fire these Martyrs I betray.
Good soules, (for you give life to every thing)
Good Angels, (for good messages you bring)
Destin'd you might have beene to such an one
As would have lov'd and worship'd you alone :
One that would suffer hunger, nakednesse,
Yea death, ere he would make your number lesse.
But, I am guilty of your sad decay;
May your few fellowes longer with me stay.

The preference of Jonson for this poem is instructive because it is typical of the time. It was this sort of thing, Donne's worst exhibitions of wire-drawn ingenuity, that formed the basis of his tremendous reputation, and that his immediate successors chose to imitate.

But if Donne had few acquaintances among the professional writers of the day he had plenty of aristocratic friends, and it was undoubtedly through their influence that he came to volunteer for the Cadiz expedition in 1596.

In that year England seemed to be in some danger. The Spanish Armada had been dispersed eight years before, and Spain showed signs of recovering from the blow. A fleet was being gathered, and a sure sign that the menace was considered serious is the fact that Elizabeth not only decided on an offensive measure, but herself contributed £50,000 and seventeen ships. The Lord Admiral Howard was in command, his lieutenants being Essex and Raleigh. Donne was in personal attendance upon Essex. His motive for joining the expedition, apart from that previously mentioned, was doubtless the desire of adventure and distinction; it seems reasonably certain also that his fortune was seriously impaired. This may have been partly due to travel and extravagance, but a letter written to his mother shows that the family fortune had been badly invested, and was in a fair way to disappear altogether. We see him, then, filled with a desire for glory and prize-money, playing his part on the " Repulse " during the victorious sea-fight before Cadiz.

As certainly did he take part in the successful land attack which Essex led in person. The expedition returned in a halo of glory, which one hopes was partly due to the presence of many of Donne's favourite 'angels.' In the following year Essex undertook another expedition. The object was to intercept the Spanish plate-ships in the neighbourhood of the Azores, but from the first ill-luck dogged the fleet. At the beginning of the voyage an exceedingly heavy storm drove the ships back to the English coast. Essex, whom Donne had again followed, took refuge in Falmouth. When the fleet finally reached the Azores no plate-ships appeared, and after various raids, in which many men were

63

lost but no gold won, the fleet returned to England. The tempest which drove back the fleet on this occasion, and a calm which delayed the ships in the tropics, were made the subject of two descriptive poems by Donne, addressed to Christopher Brooke, one of the poet's most constant friends.

These poems, although perhaps they do not deserve all the praise they have received, are nevertheless important as showing Donne's earlier manner in its most developed form. The following extract is from " The Storme."

> Then like two mighty Kings, which dwelling farre
> Asunder, meet against a third to warre,
> The South and West winds joyn'd, and, as they
>   blew,
> Waves like a rowling trench before them threw.
> Sooner then you read this line, did the gale,
> Like shot, not fear'd till felt, our sailes assaile;
> And what at first was call'd a gust, the same
> Hath now a stormes, anon a tempests name.
> *Ionas*, I pitty thee, and curse those men,
> Who when the storm rag'd most, did wake thee
>   then;
> Sleepe is paines easiest salue, and doth fullfill
> All offices of death, except to kill.
> But when I wakt, I saw, that I saw not;
> I, and the Sunne, which should teach mee had
>   forgot
> East, West, Day, Night, and I could onely say,
> If the world had lasted, now it had beene day.
> Thousands our noyses were, yet wee 'mongst all
> Could none by his right name, but thunder call:

Lightning was all our light, and it rain'd more
Then if the Sunne had drunke the sea before.
Some coffin'd in their cabins lye, equally
Griev'd that they are not dead, and yet must
    dye ;
And as sin-burd'ned soules from graves will
    creepe,
At the last day, some forth their cabbins peepe:
And tremblingly aske what newes, and doe heare
    so,
Like jealous husbands, what they would not know.
Some sitting on the hatches, would seeme there,
With hideous gazing to feare away feare.
Then note they the ships sicknesses, the Mast
Shak'd with this ague, and the Hold and Wast
With a salt dropsie clog'd, and all our tacklings
Snapping, like too-high-stretched treble strings.
And from our totterd sailes, ragges drop downe
    so,
As from one hang'd in chaines, a yeare agoe.
Even our Ordinance plac'd for our defence,
Strive to breake loose, and scape away from thence.
Pumping hath tir'd our men, and what's the gaine ?
Seas into seas throwne, we suck in againe ;
Hearing hath deaf'd our saylers ; and if they
Knew how to heare, there's none knowes what to
    say.
Compar'd to these stormes, death is but a qualme,
Hell somewhat lightsome, and the Bermuda calme.

It is only necessary to compare these verses
with those of any other poet contemporary with
Donne to see how unusual was their quality.
Instead of wrapping up his subject in gorgeous
and musical verse, Donne attempts throughout

to convey an exact idea of what he saw and experienced, and because of this constant endeavour he is the father of the poetry of reason. His contemporary admirers chose to imitate less worthy traits of his genius, but these poems stand as the prophecy and first example of that poetry of the intellect which was to dominate English literature for the better part of two centuries. They foretell it better than his lyrics, for here his passions were not engaged. When under the influence of emotion he could strike out inspired phrases and stanzas which few, if any, of his successors of the school of reason were to equal. But here he competes with them on even terms; and some surpass him. They were to subdue his harsh rhythm, and avoid his faults of taste; and so were to gain much, while losing something of his *élan*. For these poems contain some remarkably good things. In the portion of " The Storme " already quoted the opening quatrain is almost majestic, and the descriptions of the breaking rigging and flogging sails are extraordinarily vivid.

" The Calme " is, on the whole, less good, and room can be found here for only the following short passages :

Smooth as thy mistresse glasse, or what shines
    there,
The sea is now. And, as the Iles which wee
Seeke, when wee can move, our ships rooted bee.
As water did in stormes, now pitch runs out:
As lead, when a fir'd Church becomes one spout.

66

> And all our beauty, and our trimme, decayes,
> Like courts removing, or like ended playes.
> The fighting place now seamens ragges supply ;
> And all the tackling is a frippery.
> No use of lanthornes ; and in one place lay
> Feathers and dust, to day and yesterday.

There is no disputing the force of this picture, though it contains little enough of beauty. Ben Jonson was particularly struck with the last couplet. The next few lines, in which are suggested Donne's reasons for embarking on these maritime adventures, have already been referred to more than once.

> Whether a rotten state, and hope of gaine,
> Or to disuse mee from the queasie paine
> Of being belov'd, and loving, or the thirst
> Of honour, or faire death, out pusht mee first,
> I lose my end : for here as well as I
> A desperate may live, and a coward die.

A fellow-sufferer with Donne during this storm and calm was a son of Sir George Egerton, a famous lawyer, Master of the Rolls, and Lord Keeper of the Privy Seal. This young man, like Donne, was in attendance upon Essex, and doubtless our poet, who had a vast capacity for making and keeping friends, became intimate with him. This led, as a letter of the poet shows, to an introduction to the Lord Keeper. The latter, who had a keen interest in Lincoln's Inn, was probably already aware of the brilliance of Donne both as a student and a poet, and during the winter of 1597 he made him his chief secretary.

There is no question that the five years Donne spent as secretary to Egerton produced a change in his attitude to life. The Lord Keeper was both a wise man and a serious. In those days a high State appointment involved a life of considerable magnificence and outward dignity. Donne lived at York House, Egerton's residence; and the atmosphere of grave importance he found there would appeal strongly to the aristocrat in him, the more so as his own mode of life, in chambers, camps, and ships, had been anything but dignified. His duties threw him into close contact with Egerton, and so introduced him to the point of view of a man who bore a great burden of responsibility. There is evidence that Donne took to this new environment as a duck does to water, for Egerton " did always use him with much courtesy, appointing him to a place at his own table, to which he esteemed his company and discourse to be a great ornament." When five years later they parted the Lord Chancellor said, " He parted with a friend, and such a secretary as was fitter to serve a king than a subject," which is sufficient proof of the assiduity and ability Donne displayed in the course of his duties. And these duties were sufficiently important to give him (as it were, at second-hand) a taste of the sweets of position. He was the dispenser of his employer's patronage, which made him a person of

68

importance to suitors of many kinds. He would
be closely in touch with the successive measures
by which Egerton greatly increased his reputation during this period. It is highly probable
that in connexion with the most important of
these, an alliance with the Low Countries which
greatly strengthened Elizabeth's position, Donne
was sent abroad, for his verse at this time contains references to the Dutch.

It is, in fact, almost certain that Donne passed
out of the stage of reckless and arrogant re-
bellion, and attained a more mature and responsible outlook; developing at the same time
a keen ambition to enter the public service. To
this end it is extremely probable that he sub-
ordinated his private conduct, and doubtless his
memory of the ignominious circumstances of his
last entanglement encouraged him to refrain
from further experiments. It is probable that
the poem given below belongs to this time; at
any rate it displays a hesitation very much at
variance with the headlong impetuosity of
Donne's earliest period.

THE BLOSSOME

Little think'st thou, poore flower,
Whom I have watch'd sixe or seaven dayes,
And seene thy birth, and seene what every houre
Gave to thy growth, thee to this height to raise,
And now dost laugh and triumph on this bough,
Little think'st thou
That it will freeze anon, and that I shall
To morrow finde thee falne, or not at all.

JOHN DONNE & HIS POETRY

Little think'st thou poore heart
  That labour'st yet to nestle thee,
And think'st by hovering here to get a part
In a forbidden or forbidding tree,
And hop'st her stiffenesse by long siege to bow :
      Little think'st thou,
That thou to morrow, ere that Sunne doth wake,
Must with this Sunne, and mee a journey take.

  But thou which lov'st to bee
  Subtile to plague thy selfe, wilt say,
Alas, if you must goe, what's that to mee ?
Here lyes my businesse, and here I will stay :
You goe to friends, whose love and meanes present
      Various content
To your eyes, eares, and tongue, and every part.
If then your body goe, what need you a heart ?

  Well then, stay here ; but know,
  When thou hast stayd and done thy most ;
A naked thinking heart, that makes no show,
Is to a woman, but a kinde of Ghost ;
How shall shee know my heart; or having none,
      Know thee for one ?
Practise may make her know some other part,
But take my word, shee doth not know a Heart.

  Meet mee at London, then,
  Twenty dayes hence, and thou shalt see
Mee fresher, and more fat, by being with men,
Then if I had staid still with her and thee.
For Gods sake, if you can, be you so too:
      I would give you
There, to another friend, whom wee shall finde
As glad to have my body, as my minde.

But policy was the mainspring of this change in Donne's line of conduct, at any rate before 1601. The above poem, which has a very distinct poetical charm, shows that his attitude to women is as cynical as ever.

> A naked thinking heart, that makes no show,
> Is to a woman, but a kinde of Ghost.

Donne seems at this period to have been in a detached mood. The riot of passion was over for the time being, and we see him observing with cynicism, and commenting with sarcasm. A prose-work of his written during this time and called "Paradoxes and Problems" shows clearly this attitude, for one of the 'Problems' is "Why are the Fairest Falsest?" and one 'Paradox' is "That it is possible to find some Virtue in some Women." This prose-work also shows that Donne at this time was particularly interested in science and theology, which two subjects bring us to a consideration of his own poetical work of importance between 1597 and about the time of his marriage. This piece is also the only attempt he made at poetry on the large scale, and, though it remains a fragment, is the longest he ever wrote.

The preface is given in full because it gives, on unquestionable authority, a glimpse into Donne's mind. In it he is very distinctly *tête-montée*. The impudent sarcasm of the first sentence rouses one's ire, even at a distance of three centuries. It is difficult to resist the impression that Donne, in the course of his connexion with great State affairs, had forgotten that he was not plenipotentiary but secretary. He next announces that, having hitherto criticized others' work, he now offers a poem on which they may take their revenge, if they can; and especially challenges them to prove him plagiarist or unoriginal.

On this last score, indeed, he has little to fear, for the conception underlying the poem, at which he arrived by extending the Pythagorean doctrine, is startling in its anticipation of the modern theory of evolution. The idea, in a less allegorical form, is familiar enough to us, but it is hard to conceive the shock it must have given the Elizabethans, both by reason of its novelty and its impiety. It shows, however, that Donne's mind was seriously occupied by the scientific activities of the time.

INFINITATI SACRUM

16. Augusti 1601

METEMPSYCHOSIS

Poëma Satyricon

Epistle.

Others at the Porches and entries of their Buildings set their Armes; I, my picture; if any colours can deliver a minde so plaine, and flat, and through light as mine. Naturally at a new Author, I doubt, and sticke, and doe not say quickly, good. I censure much and taxe; And this liberty costs mee more then others, by how much my owne things are worse then others. Yet I would not be so rebellious against my selfe, as not to doe it, since I love it; nor so unjust to others, to do it *sine talione*. As long as I give them as good hold upon mee, they must pardon mee my bitings. I forbid no reprehender, but him that like the Trent Councell forbids not bookes, but Authors, damning what ever such a name hath or shall write. None writes so ill, that he gives not some thing exemplary, to follow, or flie. Now when I beginne this booke, I have no purpose to come into any mans debt; how my stocke will hold out I know not; perchance waste, perchance increase in use; if I doe borrow any thing of Antiquitie, besides that I make account that I pay it to posterity, with as much and as good: You shall still finde mee to acknowledge it, and to thanke not him onely that hath digg'd out treasure for mee, but that hath lighted mee a candle to the place. All which I will bid you remember, (for I will have no such Readers as I can teach) is, that the Pithagorian doctrine doth not onely carry one soule from man to man, nor man to beast, but indifferently to plants also: and therefore you must not grudge to finde the same soule in an Emperour, in a Post-horse, and in a Mucheron, since no unreadinesse in the soule, but an indisposition in the organs workes this. And therefore though this soule could not move when it was a Melon, yet it may remember, and now tell mee, at what lascivious banquet it was serv'd. And though it could not speake, when it was a spider, yet it can remember, and now tell mee, who used it for poyson to attaine dignitie. How ever the bodies have dull'd her other faculties, her memory hath ever been her owne, which makes me so seriously deliver you by her relation all her passages from her first making when shee was that apple which Eve eate, to this time when she is hee, whose life you shall finde in the end of this booke.

JOHN DONNE & HIS POETRY

The poem, which is written in a stanza of ten lines, nine of which are iambic pentameters and the last an Alexandrine, begins in the approved epic style.

I

I sing the progresse of a deathlesse soule,
Whom Fate, which God made, but doth not con-
    troule,
Plac'd in most shapes; all times before the law
Yoak'd us, and when, and since, in this I sing.
And the great world to his aged evening;
From infant morne, through manly noone I draw.
What the gold Chaldee, or silver Persian saw,
Greeke brasse, or Roman iron, is in this one ;
A worke t'outweare *Seths* pillars, bricke and stone,
    And (holy writt excepted) made to yeeld to none.

The poet then goes on to speak of himself and to outline the general plan of his work.

IV

Great Destiny the Commissary of God,
That hast mark'd out a path and period
For every thing ; who, where wee of-spring
    tooke,
Our wayes and ends seest at one instant ; Thou
Knot of all causes, thou whose changelesse brow
Ne'r smiles nor frownes, O vouch thou safe to
    looke
And shew my story, in thy eternall booke :
That (if my prayer be fit) I may understand
So much my selfe, as to know with what hand,
    How scant, or liberall this my lifes race is spand.

74

V

To my sixe lustres almost now outwore,
Except thy booke owe mee so many more,
Except my legend be free from the letts
Of steepe ambition, sleepie povertie,
Spirit-quenching sicknesse, dull captivitie,
Distracting businesse, and from beauties nets,
And all that calls from this, and to others whets,
O let me not launch out, but let mee save
Th' expense of braine and spirit; that my grave
 His right and due, a whole unwasted man may
  have.

VI

But if my dayes be long, and good enough,
In vaine this sea shall enlarge, or enrough
It selfe; for I will through the wave, and fome,
And shall, in sad lone wayes a lively spright,
Make my darke heavy Poëm light, and light.
For though through many streights, and lands I
  roame,
I launch at paradise, and I saile towards home;
The course I there began, shall here be staid,
Sailes hoised there, stroke here, and anchors laid
 In Thames, which were at Tigrys, and Euphrates
  waide.

VII

For the great soule which here amongst us now
Doth dwell, and moves that hand, and tongue, and
  brow,
Which, as the Moone the sea, moves us; to heare
Whose story, with long patience you will long ;
(For 'tis the crowne, and last straine of my song)

> This soule to whom *Luther*, and *Mahomet* were
> Prisons of flesh; this soule which oft did teare,
> And mend the wracks of th' Empire, and late
>   Rome,
> And liv'd when every great change did come,
>   Had first in paradise, a low, but fatall roome.

Stanza V is perhaps difficult, but means that unless he is guaranteed another thirty years of life free from cares of all kinds he would rather refrain from creative effort, and so avoid wearing himself out. The wish has a melancholy interest, for Destiny did not grant his prayer. Stanza VI contains in

> For though through many streights, and lands I
>   roame,
> I launch at paradise, and I saile towards home

one of these beautiful couplets which make this " darke heavy Poëm light, and light." Repetition for emphasis is a favourite trick with Donne.

Stanza VII undoubtedly refers to Queen Elizabeth. Ben Jonson told Drummond that " The conceit of Donne's Transformation or Metempsychosis was that he sought the soule of that aple which Eve pulled and thereafter made it the soule of a bitch, then of a shee wolf, and so of a woman; his generall purpose was to have brought in all the bodies of the Hereticks from the soule of Cain, and at last left in the bodie of Calvin. Of this he never wrotte but one sheet, and now, since he was made Doctor, repenteth highlie and seeketh to destroy all his poems." Either Jonson was mistaken or Donne changed his mind. The latter is more likely, for in some editions and manuscripts the clause "when shee is hee" in the last sentence of the preface reads, "when shee is shee."

This soul first appears in Paradise in an apple on the Tree of the Knowledge of Good and Evil.

IX

Prince of the orchard, faire as dawning morne,
Fenc'd with the law, and ripe as soone as borne
That apple grew, which this Soule did enlive,
Till the then climing serpent, that now creeps
For that offence, for which all mankinde weepes,
Tooke it, and t'her whom the first man did wive
(Whom and her race, only forbiddings drive)
He gave it, she, t'her husband, both did eate;
So perished the eaters, and the meate :
   And wee (for treason taints the blood) thence
     die and sweat.

X

Man all at once was there by woman slaine,
And one by one we are here slaine o'er againe
By them. The mother poison'd the well-head,
The daughters here corrupt us, Rivolets;
No smalnesse scapes, no greatnesse breaks their
     nets ;
She thrust us out, and by them we are led
Astray, from turning, to whence we are fled.
Were prisoners Judges, 'twould seeme rigorous,
Shee sinn'd, we beare; part of our paine is, thus
   To love them, whose fault to this painfull love
     yoak'd us.

XI

So fast in us doth this corruption grow,
That now wee dare aske why wee should be so.
Would God (disputes the curious Rebell) make
A law, and would not have it kept?   Or can
His creatures will, crosse his?   Of every man
For one, will God (and be just) vengeance take?
Who sinn'd?   t'was not forbidden to the snake
Nor her, who was not then made; nor is't writ
That Adam cropt, or knew the apple; yet
    The worme and she, and he, and wee endure
      for it.

XII

But snatch mee heavenly Spirit from this vaine
Reckoning their vanities, lesse is their gaine
Then hazard still, to meditate on ill,
Though with good minde; their reasons, like those
    toyes
Of glassie bubbles, which the gamesome boyes
Stretch to so nice a thinnes through a quill
That they themselves breake, doe themselves spill :
Arguing is heretiques game, and Exercise
As wrastlers, perfects them; Not liberties
    Of speech, but silence; hands, not tongues, end
      heresies.

These stanzas show us at once three of the
principal threads of this remarkable poem—
satire of women, scepticism in religion, and preoccupation with death.   In Stanza XI Donne
queries both the power and justice of God, in
XII he shows his appreciation of the futility
of theological controversy.

JOHN DONNE & HIS POETRY

Arguing is heretiques game, and Exercise
As wrastlers, perfects them.

The soul fled from the apple when the serpent
plucked it, and took up its abode in a mandrake
root, of which Sir Thomas Browne, in his
"Vulgar Errors" says: "Many . . . false conceptions there are of Mandrakes, the first from
great Antiquity, conceiveth the Root thereof
resembleth the shape of Man. . . . Now whatever encourageth the first invention, there have
not been wanting many ways of its promotion.
The first a Catachrestical and far derived
similitude it holds with Man; that is, in a bifur-
cation or division of the Root into two parts,
which some are content to call Thighs."
Hence Donne's description in the following
lines:

His right arme he thrust out towards the East,
West-ward his left; th' ends did themselves digest
Into ten lesser strings, these fingers were:
And as a slumberer stretching on his bed,
This way he this, and that way scattered
His other legge, which feet with toes upbeare.

To this spot came Eve in search of herbs to
ease her child's sickness.

Poppie she knew, she knew the mandrakes might,
And tore up both, and so coold her child's blood;
Unvirtuous weeds might long unvex'd have stood;
    But hee's short liv'd, that with his death can doe
    most good.

79

JOHN DONNE & HIS POETRY

The soul thence enters a "small blew shell," which, being hatched,

> Outcrept a sparrow, this soules moving Inne,
> On whose raw armes stiffe feathers now begin,
> As childrens teeth through gummes, to breake with
>   paine,
> His flesh is jelly yet, and his bones threds,
> All a new downy mantle overspreads,
> A mouth he opes, which would as much containe
> As his late house, and the first houre speaks
>   plaine,
> And chirps alowd for meat. Meat fit for men
> His father steales for him, and so feeds then
>   One, that within a moneth, will beate him from
>   his hen.

The sparrow, having enjoyed a short but eventful life, dies, and the soul enters the ovum of a fish. While still in an undeveloped state, it is swallowed by a swan:

> Now swome a prison in a prison put,
> And now this Soule in double walls was shut,
> Till melted with the Swans digestive fire,
> She left her house the fish, and vapour'd forth.

It finds a home again in another fish, and Donne's preoccupation with the unfairness of life, so evident throughout this poem, finds vent in a stanza which might have irked his great biographer, had he allowed himself to peruse these early indiscretions of the Dean.

> Is any kinde subject to rape like fish?
> Ill unto man, they neither doe, nor wish:

Fishers.they kill not, nor with noise awake,
They doe not hunt, nor strive to make a prey
Of beasts, nor their yong sonnes to beare away;
Foules they pursue not, nor do undertake
To spoile the nests industrious birds do make;
Yet them all these unkinde kinds feed upon,
To kill them is an occupation,
   And lawes make Fasts, and Lents for their
      destruction.

On this occasion the fish is caught by a sea-bird, which flies off with her and

Exalted she is, but to the exalters good,
As are by great ones, men which lowly stood.
   It's rais'd, to be the Raisers instrument and food.

The sea-bird is blown out to sea,

And with his prey, that till then languisht, dies:
The soules no longer foes, two wayes did erre,
The fish I follow, and keepe no calender
   Of the other; he lives yet in some great officer.

Each of these last quotations shows Donne striking at his second chief subject of satire, courtiers. The last hit is very well done. The next tenement for this soul is a whale, which is described thus:

At every stroake his brazen finnes do take,
More circles in the broken sea they make
Then cannons voices, when the aire they teare:
His ribs are pillars, and his high arch'd roofe
Of barke that blunts best steele, is thunder-proofe:
Swimme in him swallow'd Dolphins, without feare,
And feele no sides, as if his vast wombe were

F   81

> Some Inland sea, and ever as hee went
> Hee spouted rivers up, as if he ment
>   To joyne our seas, with seas above the firmament.
>
> He hunts not fish, but as an officer,
> Stayes in his court, at his owne net, and there
> All suitors of all sorts themselves enthrall;
> So on his backe lyes this whale wantoning,
> And in his gulfe-like throat, sucks every thing
> That passeth neare. Fish chaseth fish, and all,
> Flyer and follower, in this whirlepoole fall;
>
>   .   .   .   .   .
>
> Now drinkes he up seas, and he eates up flocks,
> He justles Ilands, and he shakes firme rockes.
> Now in a roomeful house this Soule doth float,
> And like a Prince she sends her faculties
> To all her limbes, distant as Provinces.

It would seem that this description must have
its origin in some bestiary, save for the 'officer'
simile. A thresher and a swordfish kill the
whale, and the soul,

>   having for her house
> Got the streight cloyster of a wreched mouse

and having been

>   late taught that great things might by lesse
>   Be slain, to gallant mischiefe doth herselfe addresse.

> Natures great master-peece, an Elephant,
> The onely harmlesse great thing; the giant
> Of beasts; who thought, no more had gone, to
>   make one wise
> But to be just, and thankfull, loth to offend,

stood sleeping, and before it hung down its
trunk,

> In which as in a gallery this mouse
> Walk'd, and surveid the roomes of this vast house,
> And to the braine, the soules bedchamber, went,
> And gnaw'd the life cords there; Like a whole towne
> Cleane undermin'd, the slaine beast tumbled downe;
> With him the murtherer dies, whom envy sent
> To kill, not scape, (for, only hee that ment
> To die, did ever kill a man of better roome,)
> And thus he made his foe, his prey, and tombe:
> Who cares not to turn back, may any whither come.

The description of the fall of the elephant is admirable, and the phrasing of the final aphorism very apt.

The soul next inhabits a wolf, which attempts to raid the flocks of "Abel, as white, and milde as his sheepe were." The sheep were safe until the wolf seduced Abel's "bitch, his sentinell," after which depredations are frequent up to the time when a trap kills the wolf. Abel's dog at this time giving birth to a litter, the soul enters a puppy, whose career was short because

> He, as his dam, from sheepe drove wolves away,
> And as his Sire, he made them his owne prey.

The soul next enters the body of an ape, which, making an attempt upon "Adams fift daughter *Siphatecia*," is killed by her brother, Tethlemite, whereupon the soul flies, and since

> Of every past shape, she knew treachery,

83

Rapine, deceit, and lust, and ills enow
To be a woman.   *Themech* she is now,
   Sister and wife to *Caine, Caine* that first did
      plow.

At this point the poet doubtless realized that, as Sir Edmund Gosse has happily put it, " at this rate of progress it would have taken millions of verses to bring us safely down to Queen Elizabeth."   He, therefore, rounds off the poem with the following outburst of dissatisfaction, and throws down his pen:

Who ere thou beest that read'st this sullen Writ,
Which just so much courts thee, as thou dost it,
Let me arrest thy thoughts ; wonder with mee,
Why plowing, building, ruling and the rest,
Or most of those arts, whence our lives are blest,
By cursed *Cains* race invented be,
And blest *Seth* vext us with Astronomie.
Ther's nothing simply good, nor ill alone,
Of every quality comparison,
   The onely measure is, and judge, opinion.

Only one critic of eminence, De Quincey, makes a high claim for " Metempsychosis."   He says that " massy diamonds compose the very substance of this poem, thoughts and descriptions which have the fervent and gloomy sublimity of Ezekiel or Æschylus."   Though many brilliant things are to be found in it, some of which have been indicated, not many will agree with this estimate.   Yet it has a certain foundation.   The original plan was majestic.   Donne

84

JOHN DONNE & HIS POETRY

proposed to indict at once Woman and God.
Woman he attacked, as is shown by the quotation from Stanza LI, by representing her as
animated by a soul which retained something
of all vices, and intended to show how it entered
naturally thereafter into heretics and evil people,
finally coming to rest in the arch-heretic John
Knox.

Donne at this time had no religious belief, but
his outlook was more or less Catholic by association. Probably, just as he was beginning to
write, however, Elizabeth executed Essex, who
was a patron of Donne, and a friend of Egerton.
Donne therefore substituted Elizabeth for John
Knox, the more willingly that she was a woman.
But in addition to his distaste for women Donne
had a bitter grievance in the general wrongness
and injustice of life, and, as the last stanza
shows, by describing how many good things
have come from " cursed Cains race " he must
have intended to question either the truth of
Christianity as it was then understood or the
wisdom of the Supreme Being.

Now these last two factors are on a much
higher plane, and, properly handled, would have
given such a poem as De Quincey describes.
And, indeed, the echoes of them, rumbling about
in the poem as it stands, give it touches of
grandeur.

> Is it of necessity
> That thousand guiltless smals, to make one great,
> must die?

But Donne was in the wrong mood. He was animated rather by cynicism than by deep sentiment, and so produced a number of satiric hits instead of a solemn indictment. At the same time his conduct of the poem was spoiled by a serious defect in construction. He deals only with the moments of exit of the soul from various bodies, so that from one point of view the poem is merely a succession of violent deaths, at once monotonous and uninspiring. In the stanzas themselves appears a fault we have met before, a lack of taste, a deficient sense of beauty. Donne could always find a vigorous description or simile, but he was as likely to choose one grotesque or disgusting as one that was beautiful.

The poem leaves with us an impression of energy, sometimes of power. We feel, too, an urge of hidden thought which never gains expression, but all these are struggling against a tide of pessimism and ugliness. It is indeed a "sullen Writ," and in being so aptly depicts Donne's state of mind. For his later life shows that he was even now at heart an idealist, craving for faith, both religious and in woman. It is easy to see from this poem that both his religious faith and his belief in woman had suffered shipwreck, and his suffering found vent in bitter sarcasm. He could not know that he was about to view some things, at any rate, from a much more pleasing angle.

86

V

THE Lady Egerton of the period when Donne joined the household was the second wife of Sir Thomas, and sister of Sir George More. The latter was Lieutenant of the Tower and a favourite of the Queen. He had much business in London, and maintained a close friendship with the Lord Keeper's family, frequently staying at York House himself, and bringing Anne, his third daughter, to visit there. In 1600 Lady Egerton died and so highly did the Lord Keeper esteem Anne, that for the time being she acted as mistress of the house. She was then barely sixteen, her duties were many and important, and she doubtless found invaluable the help of the brilliant secretary, who knew so well how to make himself attractive.

They would inevitably be thrown much together, and a mutual liking sprang up, which, aided by the curious fact that there was no woman of mature years in the household, blossomed into strong affection, and gave rise to a clandestine courtship. It is difficult to judge of Donne's conduct at this period. He must certainly be acquitted of a calculating spirit. The least deliberation would have shown him that for a secretary to entrap into marriage the daughter of a wealthy aristocrat who was under the protection of his own master was a sure way to dismissal. And Donne's post was not one to be lightly risked ; it is almost certain that Egerton would have recommended him to the Queen for promotion. What must have happened is that Donne succumbed at once to the charm of the young girl. In such case it would not be in his nature to count the cost or be conscious of anything but the object of his regard.

Donne's love for Anne More differed essentially from his previous passions. In all the poems which may reasonably be thought addressed to her there is a new note of reverence and a new absence of coarseness. It was this attachment which first set Donne's feet upon the road which led him from naturalism and a crude scepticism to mysticism and a high endeavour after faith. From this point Donne went steadily forward. He seems to have clung to his belief in his wife as to a symbol, and his chaotic outlook gradually acquired something of harmony. It is curious how this change is reflected in his verse.

The first poem which seems to be written under the influence of his new love contains all his old impetuosity and no little arrogance; it is entitled "The Canonization." He is expostulating with someone who interferes with his day-dreaming.

> For Godsake hold your tongue, and let me love,
>   Or chide my palsie, or my gout,
> My five gray haires, or ruin'd fortune flout,
>   With wealth your state, your minde with Arts
>   improve,

JOHN DONNE & HIS POETRY

Take you a course, get you a place,
Observe his honour, or his grace,
Or the Kings reall, or his stamped face
Contemplate, what you will, approve,
So you will let me love.

Alas, alas, who's injur'd by my love?
What merchants ships have my sighs drown'd?
Who saies my teares have overflow'd his ground?
When did my colds a forward spring remove?
When did the heats which my veines fill
Adde one more to the plaguie Bill?
Soldiers finde warres, and Lawyers finde out still
Litigious men, which quarrels move,
Though she and I do love.

Their tale shall be told in verse; they shall be
canonized for love; all shall address them

And thus invoke us; You whom reverend love
Made one anothers hermitage;
You, to whom love was peace, that now is rage.

No wonder Donne was absorbed. "Reverend
love," above all a love which was peace, was a
new experience for him. Here at least, his outlook is definitely changed.

The first line of this poem is deservedly
famous, and, in its kind, is equalled by Donne
only once, in the first two lines of the quatrain
from "Loves Deitie," which, though not rele-
vant, is quoted here for comparison.

I long to talke with some old lovers ghost,
Who dyed before the god of Love was borne:
I cannot thinke that hee, who then lov'd most,
Sunke so low, as to love one which did scorne.

In the next poem—*The Anniversarie*—Donne's headlong strength is subdued to the wonder of his new experience. There is in it a simplicity of diction and a delicacy—almost a bashfulness— of thought which are very charming. Donne's naturalism is fast retreating before an ideal.

The course of true love ran smoothly until toward the end of 1600, when Sir Thomas Egerton married for the third time. This meant that Anne had to leave York House, the more so as her grandfather had died, and her father, being now master of the family seat at Loseley, needed her services. The lovers had therefore to part, but not before " some faithful promises " were " so interchangeably passed as never to be violated by either party." The separation was not complete, for Anne came several times to London with her father after the Parliament met in 1601, and on each of these occasions seems to have had a private interview with Donne. During this year it became evident to those in the secret that matters were approaching a climax, and " the friends of both parties used much diligence, and many arguments to kill or cool their affections to each other : but in vain." The effect of these remonstrances on Donne was exactly what one would suppose, for in December of 1601 Anne More and he were secretly married. Christopher Brooke, whom he had first met at Oxford, and to whom he had sent " The Storme " and " The Calme," gave away the bride; Samuel Brooke, a younger brother of Christopher, officiated as priest, having just previously taken orders; another person, whose name is unknown, was present as witness. After the ceremony the bride departed to Loseley, and there for the time the matter ended.

It is safe to presume that at first Donne was filled with exultation, not only because of his marriage, but also at the unconventional manner of it. It is also clear that he later appreciated the risks he had taken. After nearly two months of very natural delay he contrived to persuade no less a person than the Duke of Northumberland to act as ambassador to his wife's father, and the Duke bore with him a letter to Sir George which contained this pithy presentment of the situation: "I know this letter shall find you full of passion; but I know no passion can alter your reason and wisdom, to which I adventure to commend these particulars; that it is irremediably done; that if you incense my lord [Egerton], you destroy her and me; that it is easy to give us happiness, and that my endeavours and industry, if it please you to prosper them, may soon make me somewhat worthier of her." The prestige of the Duke availed nothing. The letter undoubtedly found Sir George full of passion, which unfortunately altered his reason and wisdom. He challenged the adverb "irremediably" by bringing the case before the Ecclesiastical Commissioners with a plea for the dissolution of the marriage; he did his best to "destroy" them by raising such a storm that Egerton reluctantly dismissed Donne; and he flung Donne, Brooke, and the unknown witness into prison on two counts — the offence against the civil law, and for marrying a girl without her guardian's consent.

For a while Donne seems to have been in despair—with reservations. For instance, he writes abject notes to Egerton and More, yet after a letter to his wife puts " John Donne— Anne Donne—undone ! " But the Commissioners found that they could not annul the marriage; three weeks later Donne is out of prison (Christopher Brooke languished, most unjustly, in the Marshalsea at least a fortnight longer than his principal); and, most curious thing of all, by March Sir George More was begging Egerton to take back his secretary, a request to which that gentleman rightfully replied " that though he was unfeignedly sorry for what he had done, it was yet inconsistent with his place and credit to discharge and re-admit servants at the request of passionate petitioners " !

This *volte-face* of Sir George More cannot be explained without supposing powerful influence in Donne's behalf, and its source was probably the ladies of Egerton's household. His third wife was the widow of the Earl of Derby, and she had three daughters. One of these, who became in 1601 the wife of the Earl of Huntingdon, was a great friend to Donne in later years, and probably helped him at this crisis. Indeed, one of the most illuminating aspects of this episode is the revelation it gives of the esteem in which Donne, despite his subordinate position, was held. Egerton and the great ladies of his family were obviously of his party, the Duke of Northumberland acted as his envoy, Christopher Brooke, apparently without the least rancour, went to prison for him. One can only conclude that he had a most charming personality.

To the wife thus stormily won Donne remained faithful to the end. As the years passed his affection deepened. The following verses from " Loves Growth " show this change in the quality of his love, and at the same time illustrate the ceaseless analysis to which he always subjected his feelings.

> I scarce beleeve my love to be so pure
>   As I had thought it was,
>   Because it doth endure
> Vicissitude, and season, as the grasse;
> Me thinkes I lyed all winter, when I swore,
> My love was infinite, if spring make it more.
>
> .   .   .   .   .
>
> And yet no greater, but more eminent,
>   Love by the spring is growne;
>   As, in the firmament,
> Starres by the Sunne are not inlarg'd, but showne.
> Gentle love deeds, as blossomes on a bough,
> From loves awakened root do bud out now.

Strange as it may seem, nowhere is the difference in Donne's outlook more noticeable than in the dawn songs of this period. A comparison

of the following stanza from " Breake of Day "
with " The Sunne Rising," quoted previously,
will make this clear.

> Stay, O sweet, and do not rise,
> The light that shines comes from thine eyes;
> The day breaks not, it is my heart,
> Because that you and I must part.
>   Stay, or else my joys will die,
>   And perish in their infancie.

There belongs also to this period a poem which
shows that Donne had attained to a realization of the nature of true love.   This is " The
Extasie."

> Where, like a pillow on a bed,
>   A Pregnant banke swel'd up, to rest
> The violets reclining head,
>   Sat we two, one anothers best.
> Our hands were firmely cimented
>   With a fast balme, which thence did spring,
> Our eye-beames twisted, and did thred
>   Our eyes, upon one double string;
> So to entergraft our hands, as yet
>   Was all the meanes to make us one,
> And pictures in our eyes to get
>   Was all our propagation.
> As 'twixt two equall Armies, Fate
>   Suspends uncertaine victorie,
> Our soules, (which to advance their state,
>   Were gone out,) hung 'twixt her, and mee.
> And whil'st our soules negotiate there,
>   Wee like sepulchrall statues lay;
> All day the same our postures were,
>   And wee said nothing all the day.

94

JOHN DONNE & HIS POETRY

If any, so by love refin'd,
    That he soules language understood,
And by good love were growen all minde,
    Within convenient distance stood,
He (though he knew not which soule spake,
    Because both meant, both spake the same)
Might thence a new concoction take,
    And part farre purer then he came.
This Extasie doth unperplex
    (We said) and tell us what we love,
Wee see by this, it was not sexe,
    Wee see, we saw not what did move.

Yet this ethereal *heavenly* love is a more mature stage of an attachment which had its origin in a primitive passion, and our bodies are not to be despised.

We owe them thankes, because they thus,
    Did us, to us, at first convay,
Yeelded their forces, sense, to us,
    Nor are drosse to us, but allay.

.   .   .   .   .

So must pure lovers soules descend
    T'affections, and to faculties,
Which sense may reach and apprehend,
    Else a great Prince in prison lies.
To our bodies turne wee then, that so
    Weake men on love reveal'd may looke;
Loves mysteries in soules doe grow,
    But yet the body is his booke.

Donne's outlook is acquiring more harmony; he has at least solved the problem of the place in life of sex.

VI

WHEN Donne was released from prison and, the Commissioners refusing to pronounce the marriage illegal, his wife came to him, he found himself out of employment and almost without resources. We have seen from a letter to his mother that the family fortune was much reduced in value; his own portion was still further wasted by travel and extravagance. Probably it was only his salary from Egerton which had for some time kept him out of difficulties. In this extremity there came to his aid Sir Francis Woolley, who had for long been his close friend. He had just inherited an estate at Pyrford, and promptly offered the newly married people house-room. That Donne accepted the offer is significant of the state of his affairs. To Pyrford, then, he went in 1602, and remained there in close seclusion until the end of 1604. What little is known of his pursuits during this time is gathered from his correspondence. A letter to his father-in-law, who was a near neighbour, shows that a reconciliation was effected. In point of fact Sir George More gave the erring pair his blessing, but made no more substantial contribution to their happiness. During this period Donne was possibly presented to King James in the course of the monarch's visit to Sir George More. There is also extant a letter to Ben Jonson in which Donne speaks of an impending lawsuit.

96

JOHN DONNE & HIS POETRY

He probably spent most of his time in a severe course of reading, principally in theology. A letter to Robert (afterward Sir Robert) Cotton deals at length with a semi-ecclesiastical matter, and the following verses addressed to Mr Rowland Woodward show the increasingly serious bent of his mind:

> Like one who in her third widdowhood doth
>   professe
> Her selfe a Nunne, tyed to retirednesse,
> So affects my muse now, a chast fallownesse;
>
> Since shee to few, yet to too many hath showne
> How love-song weeds, and Satyrique thornes are
>   growne
> Where seeds of better Arts, were early sown.
>
> Though to use, and love Poëtrie, to mee,
> Betroth'd to no one Art, be no adulterie;
> Omissions of good, ill, as ill deeds bee.
>
> For though to us it seeme, and be light and thinne,
> Yet in those faithfull scales, where God throwes in
> Mens workes, vanity weighs as much as sinne.
>
> If our Soules have stain'd their first white, yet wee
> May cloth them with faith, and deare honestie,
> Which God imputes, as native puritie.
>
> There is no Vertue, but Religion:
> Wise, valiant, sober, just, are names, which none
> Want, which want not Vice-covering discretion.
>
>   .   .   .   .   .
>
> Wee are but farmers of our selves, yet may,
> If we can stocke our selves, and thrive, uplay
> Much, much deare treasure for the great rent day.

Manure thy selfe then, to thy selfe be approv'd,
And with vaine outward things be no more mov'd,
But to know, that I love thee and would be lov'd.

A secluded mode of life must have been very irksome to Donne. He was well known both for learning and ability in Court circles. The former is made clear by the letter to Wotton, who, being about to proceed abroad on a diplomatic mission, evidently had asked Donne, as one who could judge, the rights of the dispute about precedence between a former English ambassador and the Papal legate. The opinion held of Donne's ability is shown by Egerton's remark, which has been already quoted. In addition, the name of Jack Donne was one to conjure with as that of a wit, which was at that date the most highly esteemed qualification of all.

It seems strange at first sight that he obtained no employment, but a little thought shows two probable reasons. His family was notoriously Catholic, a fatal bar to promotion in those days, and he himself was not a member of the Church of England. A letter to Donne, the writer of which is not certainly known, but who was a close friend, contains the following sentence: "Your friends [in London] are sorry that you make yourself so great a stranger, but you best know your own occasions. Howbeit, if you have any design towards the Court, it was good you did prevent the loss of more time. . . . The King's hand is neither so full nor so open as it hath been." Almost certainly Donne's reason for not pushing his fortunes at Court was lack of money. In those days class distinctions were defended by expense in the mode of life, especially in the matter of dress, which in the upper circles was very costly. Probably, too, Donne, as the verses quoted suggest, was wrestling earnestly with the problem of his personal religion. It was his reputation as a theologian which at last obtained for him some employment.

Early in 1604 King James noted that the persecution of Puritan Nonconformists had allowed the Roman Catholics to gain much ground. He therefore requested Parliament to pass an Act tightening up the regulations regarding recusants. This they did with a will, and produced a measure so harsh that James did not wish to apply it. Instead, he issued a decree enjoining moderation, in order that "that uniformity which we desire may be wrought by clemency and by weight of reason, and not by rigour of law."

One Thomas Morton, chaplain to the Earl of Rutland, had distinguished himself by conducting controversy without the aid of invective, and he was chosen to carry out the King's campaign of persuasion. The idea was to distinguish between the different kinds of dissenters and apply suitable arguments to each. Morton's previous controversial work had been principally oral, and perhaps at first he found himself unable to write effectively and quickly, perhaps he had no time to make references and read proofs—at any rate he needed a helper. Morton had been intermittently connected for years, as chaplain, with the Hastings family, the Earls of Huntingdon, and at this time the reigning Countess was the third daughter of the Countess of Derby, Egerton's latest wife. We have seen that the ladies were good friends to Donne, and probably they recommended him to Morton. From 1605, then, to 1607 the poet was busily employed in helping to produce controversial works which were written with the object of persuading Roman Catholics that they could honestly conform to the Church of England. This work could not be done from a place so remote as Pyrford, and early in 1605 Donne and his growing family settled into a manor-house at Mitcham. The house seems to have been a poor affair —small, and with very thin walls, a terrible defect at a time when methods of heating were so imperfect. In addition, Donne had, for the purposes of his work, an apartment in the Strand. This also was a cheerless place, built over a vault, and damp. Between these two residences Donne seems from his letters to have divided his time fairly evenly, frequently riding from one to the other.

In these circumstances Donne passed two very unhappy years. He had a steadily increasing number of children, and constantly diminishing means. For some reason, either the unhealthy character of the house at Mitcham or of the Strand lodging, or because of overwork, his health became seriously impaired. His letters give abundant evidence that he was constantly preoccupied with the question of religion and that he not infrequently wished himself dead. Yet there is one incident of lighter colouring. In 1606 Donne went to France, probably to gather books or information for Morton, and his wife wished to accompany him as a page. This is the only glimpse we get of Donne's wife, who is a pathetic figure. She seems to have surrendered herself entirely to him from the first, and to have been loyal to him throughout. He took her from wealth and ease to poverty and privation; she bore him a child each year, tended him and her children through all his years of failure, and, soon after he had attained ease and position, died worn out. It is true that the picture has its gentler side. She retained her husband's love, she probably saved him from moral shipwreck, but the cost to her was very great. In 1606, however, she was no more than twenty-one, and her suggestion with regard to the journey into France shows, besides a desire to escape from Mitcham, a joy in life still unkilled. In the "Elegie on his Mistris" Donne expostulates with her :

By our first strange and fatall interview,
By all desires which thereof did ensue,
By our long starving hopes, by that remorse
Which my words masculine perswasive force

Begot in thee, and by the memory
Of hurts, which spies and rivals threatned me,
I calmly beg: But by thy fathers wrath,
By all paines, which want and divorcement hath,
I conjure thee, and all the oathes which I
And thou have sworne to seale joynt constancy,
Here I unsweare, and overswear them thus,
Thou shalt not love by wayes so dangerous.
Temper, ô faire Love, loves impetuous rage,
Be my true Mistris still, not my faign'd Page;
I'll goe, and, by thy kinde leave, leave behinde
Thee, onely worthy to nurse in my minde,
Thirst to come backe; ô if thou die before,
My soule from other lands to thee shall soare.
Thy (else Almighty) beautie cannot move
Rage from the Seas, nor thy love teach them love,
Nor tame wilde Boreas harshnesse; Thou hast
    reade
How roughly hee in peeces shivered
Faire Orithea, whom he swore he lov'd.
Fall ill or good, 'tis madnesse to have prov'd
Dangers unurg'd; Feed on this flattery,
That absent Lovers one in th' other be.
Dissemble nothing, not a boy, nor change
Thy bodies habite, nor mindes; bee not strange
To thy selfe onely; All will spie in thy face
A blushing womanly discovering grace.

This piece illustrates well one of Donne's chief
defects as a poet. The first twelve lines quoted
are admirable. From there on inspiration is left
gradually behind, and ingenuity takes its place,
with the result that toward the end the poem
trails, and becomes very artificial, as the concluding address to his wife shows. Part of it is:

102

O stay here, for, for thee
England is onely a worthy Gallerie,
To walke in expectation, till from thence
Our greatest King call thee to his presence.

One feels tempted to say that Donne never planned a poem beforehand.

The year 1607 brought with it an offer which must have caused Donne much anxious thought. By June of that year Morton's controversial campaign was finished, and he was rewarded for his success by being appointed Dean of Gloucester. Immediately after, he made Donne a proposal: "You know I have formerly persuaded you to waive your Court hopes, and enter into holy orders; which I now again persuade you to embrace, with this reason added to my former request: The King hath yesterday made me Dean of Gloucester, and I am also possessed of a benefice, the profits of which are equal to my deanery; I will think my deanery enough for my maintenance, (who am, and resolved to die, a single man) and will quit my benefice, and estate you in it, (which the patron is willing I shall do) if God shall incline your heart to embrace this motion. Remember, Mr Donne, no man's education or parts make him too good for this employment, which is to be an ambassador for the God of glory."

Two points in this offer are significant. The first is the evidence of the extreme charm of Donne's character for those who knew him well. Not lightly does any man, even a divine, share his income with another man.   The other is the indirect testimony of the last sentence quoted to Donne's reputation for learning and ability.

The offer was refused, Donne giving as reason that the open irregularities of his early life might bring scandal upon the office of priest, and that he could not satisfy himself that if he accepted the offer he would not be doing so rather to obtain a maintenance than to enhance God's glory.   His only other reason for refusal could have been a hope of obtaining a position at Court.

If the conclusion to which we shall come upon this matter be valid there is no doubt that he would rather have had secular preferment, but the fact that he had been about this time applying unsuccessfully for a post in the Queen's household proves nothing.   He was doubtless looking everywhere for employment.   His affairs were approaching a crisis, and the work with Morton was finished.   He even had to give up the rooms in the Strand, so that he was practically cut off from London.   One finds it hard to believe that in such circumstances a man as fond of his wife as Donne undoubtedly was would refuse a living equal in value to a deanery for no better reason than a vague hope of Court preferment.   Similarly, Donne's first reason can hardly have been an effective stumbling-block.   He doubtless was acutely conscious of that aspect of the case, but to refuse to follow a course sanctioned by conviction on such grounds would savour of weakness, and this book has failed signally if the reader imagines Donne weak. Almost certainly his second reason contains the germ of the matter. Undoubtedly at this time Donne was essentially a religious man. Morton had known him intimately for two years, and they had worked together on theological matters. He could not have reconciled it with his personal or professional conscience to recommend such a course to a man whom he did not know certainly to be fit for it. But to enter a Church means the acceptance of a given creed, and here Donne's intellectual honesty, which we have seen in all his verse, interfered. He had an unrivalled acquaintance with the different creeds, but he could not find in any one of them final truth. Therefore he felt he could not enter the Church.

The serious bent of Donne's mind at this time is shown by his verses to Sir Henry Goodyere, a close friend of his. This knight, who had come to Court and was dazzled into extravagance by its glitter, is given some sound advice.

Provide you manlyer dyet; you have seene
    All libraries, which are Schools, Camps, and
        Courts;
But aske your Garners if you have not beene
    In harvests, too indulgent to your sports.

Would you redeeme it? then your selfe transplant
    A while from hence. Perchance outlandish
        ground
Beares no more wit, then ours, but yet more scant
    Are those diversions there, which here abound.

To be a stranger hath that benefit,
  Wee can beginnings, but not habits choke.
Goe; whither? Hence; you get, if you forget.;
  New faults, till they prescribe in us, are smoake.

Professor Courthope says of this last stanza:
"We certainly do *not* get anything by the mere
negative act of forgetting; and nobody could
gather from the last line that the meaning was,
'New faults, till they become our masters, are
merely smoke.' Eagerness for novelty and paradox leads the poet to obscurity of expression;
and the reader is justly incensed when he finds
that the labour required to arrive at the meaning
hidden behind involved syntax and unmeasured
verse has been expended in vain." I venture
to dissent from this. Surely the verse is not
unmeasured. As to the paradox, Donne is
talking of habits, and if you forget bad habits
you do 'get' or 'gain.' Also I doubt if many
people would misread the meaning of the last
line. Certainly the quatrain contains no special
beauty, but it is not very difficult.
  Donne concludes the verses thus:

However, keepe the lively tast you hold
  Of God, love him as now, but feare him more,
And in your afternoones thinke what you told
  And promis'd him, at morning prayer before.

Let falshood like a discord anger you,
  Else be not froward. But why doe I touch
Things, of which none is in your practise new,
  And Tables, or fruit-trenchers teach as much;

> But thus I make you keepe your promise Sir,
>> Riding I had you, though you still staid there,
> And in these thoughts, although you never stirre,
>> You came with mee to Micham, and are here.

From the last stanza it would seem that Goodyere had failed to keep a promise to ride with Donne to Mitcham. Donne elsewhere mentions in a letter that he generally employed his time while riding to and fro in meditating letters to his friends.

By 1608 Donne's finances had reached a crisis. It was of little avail that his wife's family were all wealthy and well connected, and that he himself had plenty of aristocratic friends. It was simply a case of starving in the midst of plenty. His letters at this time show Donne to have been very despondent. Writing in the spring to Sir Henry Goodyere, he says:

> The pleasantness of the season displeases me. Everything refreshes, and I wither and I grow older and not better, my strength diminishes, and my load grows, and being to pass more and more storms, I find that I have . . . cast out all my ballast which nature and time gives, reason and discretion, and so am as empty and light as vanity can make me.

In August of the same year he writes:

> There is no one person but myself well of my family ; I have already lost half a child, and with that mischance of hers, my wife is fallen into such a discomposure as would afflict her too extremely,

but that the sickness of all her other children stupefies her; of one of which, in good faith, I have not much hope; and these meet with a fortune so ill provided for physic and such relief, that if God should ease us with burials, I know not how to perform even that: but I flatter myself with this hope that I am dying too; for I cannot waste faster than by such griefs. . . .

From my Hospital at Mitcham.

Donne refers frequently to fits of depression, and was beset by a tendency to suicide. It is characteristic of the straightforwardness of his intelligence that he went carefully into the subject, in order to decide whether suicide is sin. The inquiry he embodied in a pamphlet written probably with the double purpose of making clear to himself the position with regard to suicide and to free himself of the obsession by venting it. His book " Biathanatos " is, according to the title, a " Thesis, that Selfe-Homicide is not so Naturally Sinne, that it may never be otherwise." In the beginning he states that " whensoever any affliction assails me, methinks I have the keys of my prison in mine own hand, and no remedy presents itself so soon to my own heart as mine own sword." The argument is ingenious, and friends in the universities to whom he sent the book reported that they were sure that the reasoning could not be sound, yet they could discover no flaw in it. Since it was far too unorthodox to be published his writing of it seems to indicate a fear that at some time he might give way to the desire of suicide, and wished to obtain beforehand the acquittal of his own mind upon the subject—a most striking illustration of the habitual independence of his thought.

But Donne was not to be driven to any such extremity. His fortunes had reached their lowest ebb, and, but for the fact that his health seems to have suffered permanent injury during this period, deliverance from his troubles was at hand. Toward the end of 1608 the Donnes were in such a wretched state that several friends, with Sir Francis Woolley in the lead, persuaded Sir George More to pay out his daughter's dowry, and, having at last decided to move in the matter, he seems to have acted not ungenerously. He gave a bond to pay £800 on a certain day, or £20 quarterly as interest until it suited him to produce the principal. This was equivalent to an income of £800 to-day, so that food, clothes, and comforts were once more obtainable. One important result was that Donne was able again to appear in Court circles. The chief friends he made were the Countess of Bedford and Mrs Herbert, the mother of Herbert the poet. The Countess held quite a Court at Twickenham, which gave Donne the social intercourse which was so necessary to his restless mind. In return for this entertainment he wrote verses to the lady, for whom his letters show that he had a very sincere affection.

Donne seems to have met Mrs Herbert in

1607. They became fast friends, and about this time he wrote to her a series of letters which are still in existence. Later in life she became his most sympathetic helper, and he was to enjoy in her company one of the few periods of happiness which his last years afforded.

During 1609 Donne applied unsuccessfully for various posts, among them that of secretary to the new colony of Virginia. In addition he was probably occupied in preparing his " Pseudo-Martyr," which, first of all his works, was published in 1610. Its subject-matter is well indicated on the title-page: " Out of certain Propositions and Gradations, This Conclusion is evicted. That those which are of the Romane Religion in this Kingdome, may and ought to take the Oath of Allegeance." The characteristics of the book are the lawyer-like conduct of its argument, and the broad toleration of the writer's outlook. Probably Donne's early training as a Catholic and his consequent understanding of their point of view made him the very best writer that could have been chosen for such a pamphlet. The book shows little change in Donne's standpoint. He still regards religion as the question of prime importance in life; he is still looking for a solution of his theological difficulties. Signs of deep conviction are few, if any. His approach to the problem at present, though deeply earnest, is purely intellectual. The anxious thought which Donne gave to religion during these years which we have just reviewed is further indicated by occasional religious poems. These include the "Litanie," which was written during a serious illness in 1608, a poem, "The Crosse," which cannot be exactly dated, and possibly the "La Corona" sonnet sequence which will be dealt with later. The "Litanie" has little poetical merit, but shows us clearly the course of his thought. The prominent address to the Virgin Mary proves that he had not laid aside all trace of a Roman Catholic outlook.

> For that faire blessed Mother-maid,
> Whose flesh redeem'd us; That she-Cherubin,
> Which unlock'd Paradise, and made
> One claime for innocence, and disseiz'd sinne,
> Whose wombe was a strange heav'n, for
> there
> God cloath'd himselfe, and grew,
> Our zealous thankes wee poure. As her deeds were
> Our helpes, so are her prayers; nor can she sue
> In vaine, who hath such titles unto you.

His stanza on the Virgins shows that he finds all churches wanting.

> The cold white snowie Nunnery,
> Which, as thy mother, their high Abbesse, sent
> Their bodies backe againe to thee,
> As thou hadst lent them, cleane and innocent.
> Though they have not obtain'd of thee,
> That or thy Church, or I,
> Should keep, as they, our first integrity;
> Divorce thou sinne in us, or bid it die,
> And call chast widowhead Virginitie.

JOHN DONNE & HIS POETRY

It is clear that he recognizes in his intellectual arrogance a spiritual danger, for he says:

> When wee are mov'd to seeme religious
> Only to vent wit, Lord deliver us.

In this connexion also the following is significant:

> That learning, thine Ambassador,
> From thine allegeance wee never tempt,
> That beauty, paradises flower
> For physicke made, from poyson be exempt,
> That wit, borne apt high good to doe,
> By dwelling lazily
> On Natures nothing, be not nothing too,
> That our affections kill us not, nor dye,
> Heare us, weake ecchoes, O thou eare, and cry.

But the extent to which emotion was replaced by intellect in his religious outlook is best shown by "The Crosse."

> Since Christ embrac'd the Crosse it selfe, dare I
> His image, th' image of his Crosse deny?
> Would I have profit by the sacrifice,
> And dare the chosen Altar to despise?
> It bore all other sinnes, but is it fit
> That it should beare the sinne of scorning it?
> Who from the picture would avert his eye,
> How would he flye his paines, who there did dye?
> From mee, no Pulpit, nor misgrounded law,
> Nor scandall taken, shall this Crosse withdraw,
> It shall not, for it cannot; for, the losse
> Of this Crosse, were to mee another Crosse;
> Better were worse, for, no affliction,
> No Crosse is so extreme, as to have none.

Who can blot out the Crosse, which th' instrument
Of God, dew'd on mee in the Sacrament?
Who can deny mee power, and liberty
To stretch mine armes, and mine owne Crosse to be?
Swimme, and at every stroake, thou art thy Crosse;
The Mast and yard make one, where seas do tosse;
Looke downe, thou spiest out Crosses in small
    things;
Looke up, thou seest birds rais'd on crossed wings;
All the Globes frame, and spheares, is nothing else
But the Meridians crossing Parallels.

This is mere ingenuity, and the rest of the poem is worse. Here is evidently no inspiration whether of the muse or of religion, yet so diverse are the points of view of different centuries that there is little doubt that Donne's contemporaries not only acclaimed this as great poetry and imitated the manner of it, but were edified by reading it. Nor, if space permitted to quote at length from Donne's letters, and from his "Biathanatos," would the reader hesitate to conclude that Donne regarded this symbol, with which he seems to us merely to trifle in a play of wit, as representing the most serious interest in life.

VII

IN 1610 Donne found another patron in Sir Robert Drury, of Hawsted, in Suffolk. This knight enjoyed the distinction of being almost, if not quite, the wealthiest man in England, and he cherished the highest ambitions for his daughter Elizabeth. There was even talk of her marrying Prince Henry, the heir to the throne. The knight's expectations for his daughter seem to have been the measure of his affection, for when she died at the age of fifteen he was desolated with grief. Donne apparently heard of this, and—although it seems doubtful whether he had ever met Sir Robert Drury, and certainly he did not know his daughter—he wrote " A Funerall Elegie " and sent it to the distressed father. The poem contains a great deal of hyperbole, such as,

> For since death will proceed to triumph still,
> He can finde nothing, after her, to kill,
> Except the world it selfe, so great as shee,

but has one very pleasing passage of description :

> One, whose cleare body was so pure and thinne,
> Because it need disguise no thought within.
> 'Twas but a through-light scarfe, her minde
>   t'inroule ;
> Or exhalation breath'd out from her Soule.
> One, whom all men who durst no more, admir'd :
> And whom, who ere had worth enough, desir'd ;
> As when a Temple's built, Saints emulate
> To which of them, it shall be consecrate.

Never did a poem of condolence produce such satisfactory results for the author, for Drury was so grateful to Donne that " he assigned him and his wife a useful apartment in his own large house in Drury Lane, and not only rent free, but was also a cherisher of his studies, and such a friend as sympathized with him and his, in all their joy and sorrows.'' In return for all this Donne, although he may have performed duties in Drury's household, felt it incumbent upon him to show his gratitude. He produced therefore, in 1611, on the anniversary of Elizabeth Drury's death, another poem celebrating her virtues. This was called ''An Anatomie of the World: The First Anniversary,'' and was followed in 1612 by ''Of the Progresse of the Soule: The Second Anniversarie.'' Since it was obvious that two long poems could not consist entirely of lament for Elizabeth Drury, Donne made them the occasion of a full discussion of the subjects most constantly in his thought. The plan of his work is thoroughly medieval. He shows how contemptible a thing the world is, discusses the sickness into which the world is fallen, chiefly on account of Mistress Drury's death; the impossibility of its ever regaining health; points out how short is life now compared with the span of Methuselah, how small man's stature compared with the giants' of old, how all nature is similarly decayed, and how disorder rules in the world. With these dark pictures are contrasted the virtues of his subject, in whose praise he almost outpaces hyperbole.

So far the poem, except for the individual laudation made necessary by the occasion, is a stock medieval subject developed along conventional lines. It represents the orthodox opinion of his time, and is part of a view which

115

Donne was to spend agonized years in attempting to force himself to accept. But he was not purely medieval. He had the rational instinct which was the herald of a new age, and throughout this poem runs a disintegrating note of doubt, especially evoked by the new discoveries in science. The old order was passing, and Donne, unable to fit the new facts into his preconceived scheme, was too honest to pretend that they presented no difficulty. It is a hard matter to quote effectively from these two poems, but the following must serve to show how the first is conducted.

> Shee, shee is dead; shee's dead: when thou
>   knowest this,
> Thou knowest how poore a trifling thing man is.
> And learn'st thus much by our Anatomie,
> The heart being perish'd, no part can be free.
> And that except thou feed (not banquet) on
> The supernaturall food, Religion,
> Thy better Growth growes withered, and scant;
> Be more then man, or thou'rt lesse then an Ant.
> Then, as mankinde, so is the worlds whole frame
> Quite out of joynt, almost created lame:
> For, before God had made up all the rest,
> Corruption entred, and deprav'd the best:
> It seis'd the Angels, and then first of all
> The world did in her cradle take a fall,
> And turn'd her braines, and tooke a generall
>   maime,
> Wronging each joynt of th' universall frame.
> The noblest part, man, felt it first; and than
> Both beasts and plants, curst in the curse of man.

So did the world from the first houre decay,
That evening was beginning of the day,
And now the Springs and Sommers which we
    see,
Like sonnes of women after fiftie bee.
And new Philosophy calls all in doubt,
The Element of fire is quite put out;
The Sun is lost, and th' earth, and no mans wit
Can well direct him where to looke for it.
And freely men confesse that this world's spent,
When in the Planets, and the Firmament
They seeke so many new; they see that this
Is crumbled out againe to his Atomies.
'Tis all in peeces, all cohaerance gone;
All just supply, and all Relation:
Prince, Subject, Father, Sonne, are things forgot,
For every man alone thinkes he hath got
To be a Phœnix, and that then can bee
None of that kinde, of which he is, but hee.
This is the worlds condition now, and now
She that should all parts to reunion bow,
She that had all Magnetique force alone,
To draw, and fasten sundred parts in one;
She whom wise nature had invented then
When she observ'd that every sort of men
Did in their voyage in this worlds Sea stray,
And needed a new compasse for their way;
She that was best, and first originall
Of all fair copies, and the generall
Steward to Fate; she whose rich eyes, and brest
Guilt the West Indies, and perfum'd the East;
Whose having breath'd in this world, did bestow
Spice on those Iles, and bad them still smell so,
And that rich Indie which doth gold interre,
Is but as single money, coyn'd from her:

> She to whom this world must it selfe refer,
> As Suburbs, or the Microcosme of her,
> Shee, shee is dead; shee's dead: when thou knowst
>   this,
> Thou knowst how lame a cripple this world is.
> And learn'st thus much by our Anatomie,
> That this worlds generall sicknesse doth not lie
> In any humour, or one certaine part.

The first four lines of the above extract constitute a sort of refrain which Donne uses throughout the poem to mark off the episodes. It strikes very pleasantly upon the ear. The passage includes also a typical expression of doubt and some equally typical extravagant praise of Elizabeth Drury. As is usual with Donne, the poem contains one or two short passages which stand out from the rest. The best is:

> Doth not a Tenarif, or higher Hill
> Rise so high like a Rocke, that one might thinke
> The floating Moone would shipwracke there, and
>   sinke?

In the second poem, "Of the Progresse of the Soule," Donne's thought centres round a subject which since the unhappy Mitcham days has had an increasing fascination for him. From now on he shows a morbid delight in imagining the process of dissolution, and death is the main theme of this poem. Within a few lines of the beginning he introduces a gruesome simile, which is yet appallingly vivid:

Or as sometimes in a beheaded man,
Though at those two Red seas, which freely ranne,
One from the Trunke, another from the Head,
His soule be sail'd, to her eternall bed,
His eyes will twinckle, and his tongue will roll,
As though he beckned, and cal'd backe his soule,
He graspes his hands, and he pulls up his feet,
And seemes to reach, and to step forth to meet
His soule ; when all these motions which we saw,
Are but as Ice, which crackles at a thaw :
Or as a Lute, which in moist weather, rings
Her knell alone, by cracking of her strings.

In such case is the world now the "Immortall Maid" is gone, to commemorate whom it is the ambition of his muse

Yearely to bring forth such a child as this.

His efforts will inspire future wits, and so

These Hymnes thy issue, may encrease so long,
As till Gods great *Venite* change the song.

The perfection of this last line comes as a positive shock, and Professor Saintsbury says it would be his choice if he "undertook the perilous task of singling out the finest line in English sacred poetry."

Donne proceeds to exhort his soul to

Forget this rotten world ; And unto thee
Let thine owne times as an old storie bee,

which is a perfectly modulated piece of phrasing. Soon he comes back to a variant of his former refrain :

Shee, shee is gone; she is gone; when thou
　　knowest this,
What fragmentary rubbidge this world is
Thou knowest, and that it is not worth a thought;
He honors it too much that thinkes it nought.

Note the directness and force of these lines,
a sure sign that Donne's feelings are engaged.
He proceeds to a " contemplation of our state
in our death-bed," which opens with a fine
figure of Death.

Thinke then, my soule, that death is but a Groome,
Which brings a Taper to the outward roome,
Whence thou spiest first a little glimmering light,
And after brings it nearer to thy sight:
For such approaches doth heaven make in death.
Thinke thy selfe labouring now with broken
　　breath,
And thinke those broken and soft Notes to bee
Division, and thy happyest Harmonie.
Thinke thee laid on thy death-bed, loose and
　　slacke;
And thinke that, but unbinding of a packe,
To take one precious thing, thy soule from thence.
Thinke thy selfe parch'd with fevers violence,
Anger thine ague more, by calling it
Thy Physicke; chide the slacknesse of the fit.
Thinke that thou hear'st thy knell, and think no
　　more,
But that, as Bels cal'd thee to Church before,
So this, to the Triumphant Church, calls thee.
Thinke Satans Sergeants round about thee bee,
And thinke that but for Legacies they thrust;
Give one thy Pride, to another give thy Lust:

Give them those sinnes which they gave thee before,
And trust th' immaculate blood to wash thy score.
Thinke thy friends weeping round, and thinke
    that they
Weepe but because they goe not yet thy way.

The soul is exhorted to " thinke these things
cheerefully "; the "incommodities" of the soul
in the body are related; it is shown that death
gives liberty :

Thou hast thy expansion now, and libertie ;
Thinke that a rustie Peece, discharg'd, is flowne
In peeces, and the bullet is his owne,
And freely flies: This to thy Soule allow,
Thinke thy shell broke, think thy Soule hatch'd
    but now.

This passage, though vivid, is by no means
beautiful, but a little later there occurs, in a
passage on the "Immortall Maid," a most
beautiful piece of description.

Her pure, and eloquent blood
Spoke in her cheekes, and so distinctly wrought,
That one might almost say, her body thought.

All human knowledge, continues Donne, is
ignorance.   The new learning casts doubt upon
everything.

Have not all soules thought
For many ages, that our body is wrought
Of Ayre, and Fire, and other Elements?
And now they thinke of new ingredients,
And one Soule thinkes one, and another way
Another thinkes, and 'tis an even lay.

JOHN DONNE & HIS POETRY

When confined in a body the soul is told:

> Thou look'st through spectacles; small things
>   seeme great
> Below; But up unto the watch-towre get,
> And see all things despoyl'd of fallacies:
> Thou shalt not peepe through lattices of eyes,
> Nor heare through Labyrinths of eares, nor learne
> By circuit, or collections to discerne.
> In heaven thou straight know'st all, concerning it,
> And what concernes it not, shalt straight forget.

In this world the soul is brought into evil company. In heaven that is not the case. Here essential joy, which is to see God, is wanting. Even the accidental joys of heaven surpass the greatest pleasures of earth. Donne concludes with an address to the immediate occasion of the poem, in which he justifies his offering of verse.

> Since his will is, that to posteritie,
> Thou should'st for life, and death, a patterne bee,
> And that the world should notice have of this,
> The purpose, and th' authoritie is his;
> Thou art the Proclamation; and I am
> The Trumpet, at whose voyce the people came.

These poems give a rather full statement of Donne's opinions three years before he took orders. Whether these few extracts make it clear or not, the complete poems leave no doubt of the impassioned earnestness with which Donne wrote. He has a highly mystical religious ideal which involves trampling down and

122

rejecting the physical side of his nature. He
perhaps feels now, as he proved later, his ability
to achieve this, but his progress is impeded and
his faith vitiated by haunting doubts. He was,
in fact, in exactly the same difficulty as was later
the generation of Tennyson, for alone among
seventeenth-century poets he realized the full
significance of the new discoveries in astronomy,[1]
geography, and medicine. Disquiet was the
price he paid for his brilliant intellect.

The fulsome character of the adoration Donne
bestowed upon Elizabeth Drury caused much
adverse comment. The ladies of the Countess
of Bedford's circle were offended, and Ben
Jonson told Drummond that " Donne's ' Anniversarie ' was profane and full of blasphemies ;
that he told Mr Donne, if it had been written
of the Virgin Mary it had been something ;
which he answered, that he described the Idea
of a woman, and not as she [Elizabeth Drury]
was." The objections were the more widespread that Sir Robert Drury insisted on publish-
ing the poems. Their composition was clearly
due to a feeling of obligation on the part of
Donne, and the measure of effectiveness which
they possess is due, not to his subject, but to the

---

[1] Some weeks after writing the above I read in the " Morning Post " of
November 12, 1925, an article by the Very Rev. W. R. Inge, Dean of St Paul's.
In the course of a defence of a book he had recently published he says : " The
head and front of my offending seems to be that I have called attention to an
unhealed wound dealt to traditional theology at the time of the Renaissance
by the discoveries of Copernicus and Galileo. . . . There are very serious
difficulties between Science and the popular Christian view of the uni-
verse. . . ." This constitutes so significant a tribute to the penetration of
Donne that I cannot forbear quoting it.

opportunity he made in them for discussing matters of vital interest to him.

In the same year, 1612, Sir Robert and Lady Drury decided to go abroad for a time, and insisted on Donne's company. He went unwillingly, because his wife, who was then about to have a child, objected, saying, " Her divining soul boded her some ill in his absence." It was now that Donne wrote the following song, one of the few in which he combined happy diction with almost perfect unity of treatment.

SONG: SWEETEST LOVE, I DO NOT GOE

Sweetest love, I do not goe,
    For wearinesse of thee,
Nor in hope the world can show
    A fitter Love for mee;
      But since that I
Must dye at last, 'tis best,
To use my selfe in jest
    Thus by fain'd deaths to dye;

Yesternight the Sunne went hence,
    And yet is here to day,
He hath no desire nor sense,
    Nor half so short a way:
      Then feare not mee,
But beleeve that I shall make
Speedier journeyes, since I take
    More wings and spurres then hee.

O how feeble is mans power,
    That if good fortune fall,

Cannot adde another houre,
　　Nor a lost houre recall !
　　　　But come bad chance,
And wee joyne to it our strength,
And wee teach it art and length,
　　It selfe o'r us to advance.

When thou sigh'st, thou sigh'st not winde,
　　But sigh'st my soule away,
When thou weep'st, unkindly kinde,
　　My lifes blood doth decay.
　　　　It cannot bee
That thou lov'st mee, as thou say'st,
If in thine my life thou waste,
　　Thou art the best of mee.

Let not thy divining heart
　　Forethinke me any ill,
Destiny may take thy part,
　　And may thy feares fulfill ;
　　　　But thinke that wee
Are but turn'd aside to sleepe ;
They who one another keepe
　　Alive, ne'r parted bee.

Walton affirms also that the "Valediction forbidding Mourning" was composed on this occasion. It begins :

As virtuous men passe mildly away,
　　And whisper to their soules, to goe,
Whilst some of their sad friends doe say,
　　The breath goes now, and some say, no :

So let us melt, and make no noise,
　　No teare-floods, nor sigh-tempests move,
T'were prophanation of our joyes
　　To tell the layetie our love.

JOHN DONNE & HIS POETRY

In the later stanzas he develops the famous simile of the compasses, which his contemporaries valued so highly. This is an excellent illustration of the contention already advanced that Donne could not distinguish between a parallel which was merely exact and one which was also beautiful. Certainly in this case his conception of beauty was mathematical.

Our two soules therefore, which are one,
  Though I must goe, endure not yet
A breach, but an expansion,
  Like gold to ayery thinnesse beate.

If they be two, they are two so
  As stiffe twin compasses are two,
Thy soule the fixt foot, makes no show
  To move, but doth, if the other doe.

And though it in the center sit,
  Yet when the other far doth rome,
It leanes, and hearkens after it,
  And growes erect, as that comes home.

Such wilt thou be to mee, who must
  Like th' other foot, obliquely runne;
Thy firmnes makes my circle just,
  And makes me end, where I begunne.

Of this journey Walton records an instance, which known facts seem to confirm, of thought transference. He says: "Two days after their arrival there, Mr Donne was left alone in that room in which Sir Robert, and he, and some other friends had dined together. To this place Sir Robert returned within half an hour; and as he left, so he found, Mr Donne alone; but in such an ecstasy, and so altered as to his looks, as amazed Sir Robert to behold him; insomuch that he earnestly desired Mr Donne to declare what had befallen him in the short time of his absence. To which Mr Donne was not able to make a present answer; but, after a long and perplexed pause, did at last say: ' I have seen my dear wife pass twice by me through this room, with her hair hanging about her shoulders, and a dead child in her arms: this I have seen since I saw you.' '' A messenger sent post haste to England returned with the information that a dead child had indeed been born '' the same day and about the very hour that Mr Donne affirmed he saw her pass by him in his chamber.''

Before visiting Paris the travellers had stayed in Amiens. Donne's letters show that from Paris, where he fell ill, they went to Spa, and after journeying through the Spanish Netherlands returned to England. During this journey Donne wrote a good deal of complimentary verse to various ladies. The most interesting of these efforts is that given below, for it contains a direct and humble apology for his extravagant praise of Elizabeth Drury.

TO THE COUNTESSE OF BEDFORD
Begun in France but never perfected

Though I be *dead*, and buried, yet I have
  (Living in you,) Court enough in my grave,
As oft as there I thinke my selfe to bee.
  So many resurrections waken mee.

That thankfullnesse your favours have begot
  In mee, embalmes mee, that I doe not rot.
This season as 'tis Easter, as 'tis spring,
  Must both to growth and to confession bring
My thoughts dispos'd unto your influence ; so,
  These verses bud, so these confessions grow.
First I confesse I have to others lent
  Your stock, and over prodigally spent
Your treasure, for since I had never knowne
  Vertue or beautie, but as they are growne
In you, I should not thinke or say they shine,
  (So as I have) in any other Mine.
Next I confesse this my confession,
    For, 'tis some fault thus much to touch
      upon
Your praise to you, where half rights seeme too
      much,
    And make your minds sincere complexion
      blush.
Next I confesse my impenitence, for I
    Can scarce repent my first fault, since thereby
Remote low Spirits, which shall ne'r read you,
    May in lesse lessons finde enough to doe,
By studying copies, not Originals,

            Desunt cætera.

Donne was now forty years old, and without
a dependable source of income. His wife's
allowance from her father and the hospitality of
Sir Robert Drury made his mode of life comfortable, even luxurious. But it was exceedingly
precarious, being dependent upon the whim of
a patron and the resources of a most extravagant
father-in-law. We find, therefore, in Donne
128

during the next two years an extreme anxiety to stabilize his position. This desire not only led him to an assiduous petitioning of Court favourites, a thing in itself distasteful to our age, but into baser ways, in which we can see him walk only with profound regret. Of his constant begging letters to courtiers asking their recommendation for various posts ranging from obscure ones in the royal household to that of Ambassador to Venice little need be said. Such solicitation was the only means of approach to princes, and the subservient tone of the letters is largely a matter of the conventional phraseology of the time. Besides, Donne was sufficiently distinguished to have a claim. His being commissioned to write the marriage-song for the Princess Elizabeth and the Elector Palatine is guarantee enough of this. In epithalamia Donne was perhaps more consistently successful than in any other kind. He wrote three. The first belongs to his Lincoln's Inn days, and shows its date in its audacity and a familiar pun.

Daughters of London, you which bee
Our Golden Mines, and furnish'd Treasurie,
    You which are Angels, yet still bring with you
Thousands of Angels on your mariage daies.

For all that it is an energetic and a tuneful poem. That addressed to the Princess Elizabeth is, however, a much finer piece of work. The marriage took place on St Valentine's Day, 1612. The following is Donne's opening stanza :

I   .   129

Haile Bishop Valentine, whose day this is,
    All the Aire is thy Diocis,
    And all the chirping Choristers
And other birds are thy Parishioners,
      Thou marryest every yeare
The Lirique Larke, and the grave whispering
    Dove,
The Sparrow that neglects his life for love,
The household Bird, with the red stomacher,
    Thou mak'st the black bird speed as soone,
As doth the Goldfinch, or the Halcyon;
The husband cocke lookes out, and straight is sped,
And meets his wife, which brings her feather-bed.
This day more cheerfully then ever shine,
This day, which might enflame thy self, Old
    Valentine.

This is really melodious and gay—the latter being an effect seldom found in Donne.

To his attempts to obtain a Court post through the influence of Lord Hay and other friends no exception can be taken. It was the only course open to him. From the practice of law he was debarred because, although he had profound knowledge in it, he had never qualified, and the Church had been closed to him on account of his refusal to take orders. It was unthinkable that he, poet and wit, brother-in-law to knights and lords, should adopt any plebeian method of earning a living. Yet his need of security was acute, and he adopted a distinctly unsavoury method of attaining it.

At the end of 1612 Frances Howard, Countess of Essex, commenced proceedings to divorce her husband. Her object was a marriage with Rochester, the all-powerful favourite. Now Donne had some time before written to Rochester announcing his intention of taking orders and soliciting his patronage. Rochester evidently dissuaded him from entering the Church, and promised secular advancement if he would help to put through the divorce proceedings. Donne wrote to a friend "concerning this nullity":

My poor study having lain that way, it may prove possible that my weak assistance may be of use in this matter in a more serious fashion than an epi-thalamium. This made me therefore abstinent in that kind; yet, by my troth, I think I shall not escape. I deprehend in myself more than an alacrity, a vehemency to do service to that company, and so I may find reason to make rhyme.

From this it appears that he was contemplating with equanimity not only the task of furthering a scandalous divorce, but also that of writing a marriage-song for a woman who at present was the wife of another man than his patron. Of course, it must be remembered that at first Donne was probably unaware of the worst features of the case, for the charge against the Countess of Essex of having attempted to murder her husband was not brought forward until the proceedings had commenced, but the above letter shows that he knew from the beginning the true reason for the action being laid.

JOHN DONNE & HIS POETRY

After considerable delay the suit was granted; Rochester, created Earl of Somerset for the occasion, married the lady, and Donne produced his marriage-song " Ecclogue : 1613, December 26 ". The epithalamium, which is set in a dialogue between the writer " Idios," the private man—*i.e.*, one who holds no place at Court—and a friend, is much too good for the occasion. The following stanzas must suffice to show its movement :

Her Apparrelling

Thus thou descend'st to our infirmitie,
 Who can the Sun in water see.
 Soe dost thou, when in silke and gold,
Thou cloudst thy selfe ; since wee which doe
  behold,
 Are dust, and wormes, 'tis just
Our objects be the fruits of wormes and dust ;
Let every Jewell be a glorious starre,
Yet starres are not so pure, as their spheares are.
And though thou stoope, to appeare to us in part,
Still in that Picture thou intirely art,
Which thy inflaming eyes have made within his
 loving heart.

Going to the Chappell

Now from your Easts you issue forth, and wee,
 As men which through a Cipres see
 The rising sun, doe thinke it two,
Soe, as you goe to Church, doe thinke of you,
  But that vaile being gone,
By the Church rites you are from thenceforth one.

JOHN DONNE & HIS POETRY

The Church Triumphant made this match before,
And now the Militant doth strive no more;
Then, reverend Priest, who Gods Recorder art,
Doe, from his Dictates, to these two impart
All blessings, which are seene, or thought, by
    Angels eye or heart.

The wedding took place in December 1613. All that remained was for Somerset to find for Donne the promised 'place,' but this he was slow to do.

During this time Donne was in a bad state of health. We have seen that in the course of his travels on the Continent in 1612 he was seriously ill with fever. In 1613 he had a further attack, and, worst of all, was threatened with blindness. For some time he could see very little, but his eyes gradually recovered. Meanwhile Somerset showed no sign of keeping the bargain, and when six months had passed without any reward Donne's letters began to lay aside their servility and urge their case in more direct terms. The cause of this was perhaps not only the delay; it is probable that Donne, who knew so well how to interpret straws on Court waters, became convinced that the King was tiring of Somerset. At last the latter, when nearly a year was passed, summoned Donne to attend the King. As the poet was on his way to Theobalds in Hertfordshire he little thought what would be the nature of the preferment offered him. When he reached his destination Somerset met him and told him that one of the clerks of the Council had died the night before. Donne probably hinted that, judging from previous experience, it did not follow as the night the day that he would become thereby a clerk to the Council, for Somerset replied: " 'Mr Donne, to testify the reality of my affection, and my purpose to prefer you, stay in this garden till I go up to the King, and bring you word that you are clerk to the Council: doubt not my doing this, for I know the King loves you, and know the King will not deny me.' But the King gave a positive denial to the request and, having a discerning spirit, replied: 'I know Mr Donne is a learned man and has the abilities of a learned divine, and will prove a powerful preacher; and my desire is to prefer him that way, and in that way I will deny you nothing for him.' " And so the matter was virtually settled, for the King was really anxious for Donne to enter the Church. The latter merely reserved his decision for a few days in order to consult his friends, then repaired to the King at Newmarket, where he made a statement of his views and scruples, which were graciously considered by James. He thereupon decided to take orders, receiving from the King " as good allowance and encouragement to pursue my purpose as I could desire."

The letter from which the last quotation is made was written on the following day, and shows Donne already busy with his preparations. In it he makes anxious inquiry about the attitude of Abbot, Archbishop of Canterbury, to Somerset.

The Archbishop had been a bitter opponent of the divorce of the Countess of Essex, and though Donne's part in the proceedings had doubtless been kept secret, the source of the Countess's brilliant legal advice would probably be clear enough to his Grace from the moment that Somerset tried to obtain preferment for Donne; at any rate, he would know that Donne was a follower of the Earl, whom Abbot cordially detested. Donne, therefore, resorting to the wisdom of the serpent, sent him certain '' Essays on Divinity,'' which give indeed ample proof of his orthodoxy and learning, but have few traces of deep personal conviction. It is very doubtful if Abbot was ever won over, else Donne, who became admittedly the most eloquent, the most learned, and the most saintly of contemporary divines, would certainly at some time have been awarded a bishopric. Before leaving secular life Donne proposed to print his poems, and in his letters we find him busy collecting them. No copy of this edition is extant, probably because it was never printed. His friends and his own common sense must surely have pointed out that the works of Jack Donne the wit would hardly be a satisfactory blazon for John Donne the divine.

He was ordained toward the end of January 1615, and it seems probable that he held for a while a curacy at Paddington, where he certainly preached his first sermon.

VIII

TO say that, at the time of his taking orders, Donne was a Christian in the most complete conception of the word, which involves self-sacrifice, a persuasion of communion with God, and abhorrence of the world, would certainly be a misstatement. Yet he was a man of moral life, having a grave sense of the importance of religion, one of the best theologians in England, and possessed of great ability. King James was right in judging that Donne would make a learned and capable divine. Having taken the plunge he applied himself unsparingly to his new calling. At first he was very diffident about preaching; one would say it was the first time he had ever experienced the sensation. He chose country churches such as St Pancras for his early efforts, and within a month or two preached before the Queen. When later in the year he delivered a sermon at Whitehall his success was assured. The King was more than satisfied, made Donne his chaplain, and within twelve months promotions began to pour in. The King forced Cambridge, much against its will, to confer on Donne the degree of Doctor of Divinity. The objection of the university seems to have been based partly on academic jealousy, for Donne in 1610 had been made honorary M.A. of Oxford, partly on policy, because degrees had been given away far too freely in past years, and partly on honest doubt

136

whether Jack Donne the wit could become in so few months a worthy recipient. In 1616 the livings of Keyston and Sevenoaks were bestowed on the newly made Doctor. He continued to reside in London, of course. There was no nonsense in those days about pluralities and absentee landlords. Of these livings Sevenoaks, at any rate, was richly endowed, so that from this time Donne's financial troubles were over.

A further appointment in this year probably gratified him a great deal. He was made Divinity Reader to the Benchers of Lincoln's Inn. This certainly was no sinecure, for he had to deliver fifty sermons a year, each one hour long, before the most learned and critical audience in England. By the end of 1616 Donne's financial position was assured; he was famous for his preaching, and on the highroad to further promotion, which there is little reason to doubt he eagerly coveted.

Fate in 1617 dealt him a blow from which his ambition never entirely recovered. His wife died of sheer weakness after giving birth to her twelfth child. To us she appears the uncomplaining sacrifice to his egotism, and one can hardly believe she can have been sorry to be rid of the burden of life. But to Donne, whose love for her was as real as it was selfish, the loss was a terrible blow.

It was his love for her that had rescued him from the bitterness of hopeless scepticism; it was his affection for and belief in this gentle, compliant lady which had constantly confirmed his faith in good, and such faith is a necessary preliminary to belief in God. Arguing from her nature and the nature of those like her, he had come to believe in God. But until her death his belief had been purely intellectual. He considered it sincere, but, having domestic affection and many interests, he had felt no need of it as a prop. Now everything was changed. His wife had gone, and he felt an intense loneliness. His world lay shattered at his feet, mere pleasures were ashes in his mouth. In his distress he turned to his God, not as a theoretical deity whom his theology told him must exist, but as an almighty source of comfort with whom he longed to place himself in personal communion. For this comforting assurance he wrestled with all the might of his vast egotism. In the course of the struggle he seems to have passed through all phases but the last of what is generally called 'conversion.' It is almost certain, however, that he never succeeded in attaining his end— a *continual* consciousness of the comforting presence of God within him.

The reason for this failure was the conflicting elements of his nature. The idealist in him longed for God, and he conceived God after the manner of his generation, largely according to the teaching of the Roman Catholic *milieu* in which he had passed his youth. Given the information of his time, there was no other view open to him. But his virile intellect—that

138

intellect which made him, alone among the poets of his day, realize that the new discoveries struck at the root of the accepted fabric of religious thought—refused to make some of the vast assumptions which the contemporary view of God required. The urgency of his spiritual need of God and his latent scepticism were sufficient in themselves to cause a tremendous struggle within him, but the keenness of desperation was imparted to it by his horror of death. We have noted before how the subject of death was gaining an increasing hold on his imagination. From this time forth it seems constantly with him. It was not merely terror, although undoubtedly that formed one factor, but the gruesome circumstances of decay which held him in morbid fascination.

Donne's inconclusive agony of soul is set forth in full in the "Holy Sonnets," nineteen in number, which were composed just after the death of his wife. These form the most important body of verse that he wrote after entering the Church. When he strives to turn to God for comfort he realizes acutely his unworthiness, the weight of sin that he bears.

HOLY SONNETS

IV

Oh my blacke Soule ! now thou art summoned
By sicknesse, deaths herald, and champion ;
Thou art like a pilgrim, which abroad hath done
Treason, and durst not turne to whence hee is fled,

Or like a thiefe, which till deaths doome be read,
Wisheth himselfe delivered from prison ;
But damn'd and hal'd to execution,
Wisheth that still he might be imprisoned.
Yet grace, if thou repent, thou canst not lacke ;
But who shall give thee that grace to beginne?
Oh make thy selfe with holy mourning blacke,
And red with blushing, as thou art with sinne ;
Or wash thee in Christs blood, which hath this
    might
That being red, it dyes red soules to white.

Viewing his life forward and back, he realizes
how short a term remains to him, and utters
this cry—the close-packed verse indicates its
urgency :

VI

This is my playes last scene, here heavens
    appoint
My pilgrimages last mile ; and my race
Idly, yet quickly runne, hath this last pace,
My spans last inch, my minutes latest point,
And gluttonous death, will instantly unjoynt
My body, and soule, and I shall sleepe a space,
But my ever-waking part shall see that face,
Whose feare already shakes my every joynt :
Then, as my soule, to heaven her first seate, takes
    flight,
And earth-borne body, in the earth shall dwell,
So, fall my sinnes, that all may have their right,
To where they are bred, and would presse me, to
    hell.
Impute me righteous, thus purg'd of evill,
For thus I leave the world, the flesh, the devill.

He knows that before remission of sins is possible there must be repentance.

VII

At the round earths imagin'd corners, blow
Your trumpets, Angells, and arise, arise
From death, you numberlesse infinities
Of soules, and to your scattred bodies goe,
All whom the flood did, and fire shall o'erthrow,
All whom warre, dearth, age, agues, tyrannies,
Despaire, law, chance, hath slaine, and you whose
    eyes,
Shall behold God, and never tast deaths woe.
But let them sleepe, Lord, and mee mourne a
    space,
For, if above all these, my sinnes abound,
'Tis late to aske abundance of thy grace,
When wee are there; here on this lowly ground,
Teach mee how to repent; for that's as good
As if thou hadst seal'd my pardon, with thy
    blood.

But even upon his self-abasement his doubting intellect intrudes, to be rejected immediately in a storm of contrition.

IX

If poysonous mineralls, and if that tree,
Whose fruit threw death on else immortall us,
If lecherous goats, if serpents envious,
Cannot be damn'd; Alas; why should I bee?
Why should intent or reason, borne in mee,
Make sinnes, else equall, in mee more heinous?
And mercy being easie, and glorious

To God; in his sterne wrath, why threatens
    hee?
But who am I, that dare dispute with thee
O God?   Oh! of thine onely worthy blood,
And my teares, make a heavenly Lethean flood,
And drowne in it my sinnes blacke memorie;
That thou remember them, some claime as debt,
I thinke it mercy, if thou wilt forget.

Sonnet XI shows, in the horror of sin which his references to Christ in the latter part indicate, that he has attained to true repentance as distinct from fear of consequences.

XI

Spit in my face you Jewes, and pierce my side,
Buffet, and scoffe, scourge, and crucifie mee,
For I have sinn'd and sinn'd, and onely hee,
Who could do no iniquitie, hath dyed:
But by my death can not be satisfied
My sinnes, which passe the Jewes impiety:
They kill'd once an inglorious man, but I
Crucifie him daily, being now glorified.
Oh let mee then, his strange love still admire:
Kings pardon, but he bore our punishment.
And *Iacob* came cloth'd in vile harsh attire
But to supplant, and with gainfull intent:
God cloth'd himselfe in vile mans flesh, that so
Hee might be weake enough to suffer woe.

Despite a net of paradoxical images, Sonnet XIV expresses adequately, in its striking metaphor and its forceful diction, his burning desire for an assurance of forgiveness.

XIV

Batter my heart, three person'd God; for, you
As yet but knocke, breathe, shine, and seeke to
    mend;
That I may rise, and stand, o'erthrow mee, and
    bend
Your force, to breake, blowe, burn and make me
    new.
I, like an usurpt towne, to another due,
Labour to admit you, but Oh, to no end,
Reason your viceroy in mee, mee should defend,
But is captiv'd and proves weake or untrue.
Yet dearely I love you, and would be loved faine,
But am betroth'd unto your enemie:
Divorce mee, untie, or breake that knot againe,
Take mee to you, imprison mee, for I
Except you enthrall mee, never shall be free,
Nor ever chast, except you ravish mee.

But, apart from a single couplet in the sonnet
which, by its reference to his wife, dates the
series,

But though I have found thee, and thou my thirst
    hast fed,
A holy thirsty dropsy melts mee yett,

the concluding sonnets show that he did not
attain at this time to any permanent satisfaction.

XIX

Oh, to vex me, contraryes meet in one:
Inconstancy unnaturally hath begott
A constant habit; that when I would not

JOHN DONNE & HIS POETRY

I change in vowes, and in devotione.
As humorous is my contritione
As my prophane Love, and as soone forgott:
As ridlingly distemper'd, cold and hott,
As praying, as mute; as infinite, as none.
I durst not view heaven yesterday; and to day
In prayers, and flattering speaches I court God:
To morrow I quake with true feare of his rod.
So my devout fitts come and go away
Like a fantastique Ague: save that here
Those are my best dayes, when I shake with
    feare.

And if Donne could achieve no stability, no
permanent hold of the ecstatic adoration which
was his soul's ideal, his intellect was no less un-
certain in the matter of theology. Sonnet XVIII
proves that he was quite undecided which one,
and unconvinced that any one of the three great
Churches—the Roman Catholic, the Genevan,
and the English—could make good its claim to
be absolute truth.

XVIII

Show me deare Christ, thy spouse, so bright and
    clear.
What! is it She, which on the other shore
Goes richly painted? or which rob'd and tore
Laments and mournes in Germany and here?
Sleepes she a thousand, then peepes up one
    yeare?
Is she selfe truth and errs? now new, now outwore?
Doth she, and did she, and shall she evermore
On one, on seaven, or on no hill appeare?

Dwells she with us, or like adventuring knights
First travaile we to seeke and then make Love?
Betray kind husband thy spouse to our sights,
And let myne amorous soule court thy mild
   Dove,
Who is most trew, and pleasing to thee, then
When she is embrac'd and open to most men.

Donne's doubt as to where the truth lay between the claims of the various churches is probably the main reason for his notable tolerance, a virtue conspicuously lacking in the clergy of this time. A man not too certain of his own convictions, and capable, through early training, of appreciating the point of view of dissenters, has weighty reason for abstaining from arrogant dogma.

Apart from the "Holy Sonnets" the most considerable portion of Donne's "Divine Poems" is a series of seven sonnets, called "La Corona." The date of these is a famous crux. What evidence there is rather suggests that they were written in 1607, but much conjecture is needed to make it suggest anything, and it is better to retain an open mind on the subject. The versification tends to convince one that they were written at least as late as the "Holy Sonnets," that is, not before 1617. We noted long since that in his early days Donne signalized his revolt from convention in verse by refusing to use all the most popular measures of his day, and by substituting in his verse deliberate discord for harmony. Inquiry will show that this phase

JOHN DONNE & HIS POETRY

gradually passed. As he grew older he used
more conventional metres, and his verse became smoother, until in his middle period very
few discords appear, if he be read carefully.
Coleridge was the first to note this fact. He
points out that Donne has two methods of hand-
ling rhythm. In songs and purely lyrical pieces
he arranges the words so that the stresses fall
correctly whether the sense be much regarded
or not ; but in poems where he is thinking, and
expects the reader to think, the sense emphasis
has to be made for the verse to run properly.
When allowance is made for the shockingly
corrupt state of the manuscripts this disposes of
the contention that Donne had no ear. In "The
Satyres," of course, his verse is rugged of set
purpose. By the time we reach his last period,
that of the " Divine Poems," it is only seldom
that Donne exacts of his reader the tribute of
paying attention to his meaning. There is but
one example (line 9) in the sonnet from " La
Corona " quoted below. The rest runs smoothly ;
in fact, there is something seductive about the
movement of this series, in spite of the rime-
closed couplet at the end, which always, even in
Shakespeare, feels like a sigh of relief for a
finished task. Perhaps the impression of melody
is increased by the device of connecting each
sonnet with the previous one by repeating the
last line with a change of accent.

LA CORONA

I

Deigne at my hands this crown of prayer and praise,
Weav'd in my low devout melancholie,
Thou which of good, hast, yea art treasury,
All changing unchang'd Antient of dayes;
But doe not, with a vile crowne of fraile bayes,
Reward my muses white sincerity,
But what thy thorny crowne gain'd, that give mee,
A crowne of Glory, which doth flower alwayes;
The ends crowne our workes, but thou crown'st
    our ends,
For, at our end begins our endlesse rest;
The first last end, now zealously possest,
With a strong sober thirst, my soule attends.
'Tis time that heart and voice be lifted high,
Salvation to all that will is nigh.

It may seem at first sight curious that Donne turned to the sonnet for his religious poetry. Yet it will be seen from his work that the instinctive artist in him chose measures suitable to the various types of poetry which he attempted —a harsh couplet for satire, a smooth one for complimentary verse, a sonorous stanza for the "Metempsychosis." By the time he came to write the "Divine Poems" he was long past the stage of avoiding a measure merely because it was popular. His own thought was mature, and his ideas had dissociated and become clear cut. It is unity of idea above everything that the sonnet form demands, and Donne doubtless felt its appropriateness to divinity, which abounds in conceptions capable, for the purposes of poetry, of being isolated. The " La Corona " series conveys a satisfying completeness, dealing as it does with points in Christ's career, the " Annunciation," " Nativity," " Temple," " Crucifying," " Resurrection," " Ascension." This effect is increased by the interlinking already mentioned. The line which begins and ends the series is very attractive :

Deigne at my hands this crown of prayer and praise.

Very appropriate too is the epithet of 'sincerity ' in

But doe not, with a vile crowne of fraile bayes,
Reward my muses white sincerity.

The poetical standard of the whole is not high, but the last sonnet ends in an address much finer than the rest.

O strong Ramme, which hast batter'd heaven for
    mee,
Mild Lambe, which with thy blood, hast mark'd
    the path ;
Bright Torch, which shin'st, that I the way may
    see,
Oh, with thy owne blood quench thy owne just
    wrath,
And if thy holy Spirit, my Muse did raise,
Deigne at my hands this crowne of prayer and praise.

The " Holy Sonnets," which have been much more freely quoted here, though they lack the surface completeness of " La Corona," and seem perhaps a little less carefully written, contain several things which far surpass any part of the latter series. The best of all is Sonnet VII, already quoted. The development of the idea is perfectly modulated, the movement of the octet is so dignified as to be almost Miltonic, and the normal effect of the last couplet is avoided by the happy device of beginning the period in the middle of the twelfth line. In the next sonnet he says that his

> fathers soule doth see,
> And adds this even to full felicitie,
> That valiantly I hels wide mouth o'rstride.

Images like this last assure Donne of his place, in spite of much which is mere ingenuity.

Donne continued with his preaching before the King, Queen, and the Benchers until 1619, when he was so worn down by work and continual inward struggle that he was thought to be in a decline.

The King therefore appointed him chaplain to Lord Hay, who was going into Germany as ambassador. After his appointment there was a period of delay before starting, during which Donne wrote "A Hymne to Christ."

A HYMNE TO CHRIST, AT THE AUTHOR'S LAST GOING INTO GERMANY

> In what torne ship soever I embarke,
> That ship shall be my embleme of thy Arke;
> What sea soever swallow mee, that flood
> Shall be to mee an embleme of thy blood;

JOHN DONNE & HIS POETRY

Though thou with clouds of anger do disguise
Thy face; yet through that maske I know those
  eyes,
  Which, though they turne away sometimes,
    They never will despise.

I sacrifice this Iland unto thee,
And all whom I lov'd there, and who lov'd
  mee;
When I have put oùr seas twixt them and mee,
Put thou thy sea betwixt my sinnes and thee.
As the trees sap doth seeke the root below
In winter, in my winter now I goe,
  Where none but thee, th' Eternall root
    Of true Love I may know.

Nor thou nor thy religion dost controule,
The amorousnesse of an harmonious Soule,
But thou would'st have that love thy selfe: As
  thou
Art jealous, Lord, so I am jealous now,
Thou lov'st not, till from loving more, thou free
My soule: Who ever gives, takes libertie:
  O, if thou car'st not whom I love
    Alas, thou lov'st not mee.

Seale then this bill of my Divorce to All,
On whom those fainter beames of love did fall;
Marry those loves, which in youth scattered bee
On Fame, Wit, Hopes (false mistresses) to thee.
Churches are best for Prayer, that have least
  light:
To see God only, I goe out of sight:
  And to scape stormy dayes, I chuse
    An Everlasting night.

150

JOHN DONNE & HIS POETRY

This poem is remarkable as showing the smoothness and harmony of Donne's versification in his last period. The imagery has another interest. It has been frequently remarked that when Donne took orders he did not abandon wit and the subjects of wit, but turned them to spiritual purposes. This poem is composed of wit and the language of love, both addressed to God. It is an etherealized version of such a song as might be offered to a mistress, and is important because this "amorousnesse" in religion was imitated very freely by his successors.

The travels of the embassy lasted from May 1619 until January 1620. The duties of the chaplain were to ride in the most luxurious fashion possible in the train of the ambassador, or rather, since Lord Hay was one of Donne's most intimate friends, in his company; to consult with him about the course of diplomacy to be followed; and very occasionally to preach before a Court. No better holiday for Donne could have been desired, for not only did he have rest from work, but the experience of visiting little-known parts of Europe would appeal to his intelligence and insatiable curiosity, and prevent brooding over the spiritual trouble which had of late obsessed him. Returning strengthened in mind and body, he resumed his duties, and for a while we catch glimpses of the old assertive Donne. For instance, he attempted to obtain a deanery which fell vacant, but was

151

unsuccessful. This disappointment the King made up to him in 1621 by appointing him Dean of St Paul's. Walton relates the incident in a very pleasing way:

The King sent to Dr Donne, and appointed him to attend him at dinner the next day. When his Majesty was sat down, before he had eat any meat, he said after his pleasant manner, "Dr Donne, I have invited you to dinner, and, though you sit not down with me, yet I will carve to you of a dish that I know you love well; for, knowing you love London, I do therefore make you Dean of St Paul's; and when I have dined, then do you take your beloved dish home to your study, say grace there to yourself, and much good may it do you."

But Donne had to wait until the end of the year for his meal. Archbishop Abbot, when hunting, accidentally killed a man with an arrow, and no promotions could be made until a commission had decided whether an archbishop who had killed a man, even accidentally, could continue to hold office. Judgment was awarded in the Archbishop's favour, the ecclesiastical machine was set in motion again, the then Dean of St Paul's was consecrated bishop, and Donne succeeded to the deanery. The office was very suitable to him; it gave him a place at Court, was a prominent position, and kept him in close touch with London. Donne, like most of his contemporaries, was firmly persuaded that he loved London and hated the country. One result of the new appointment was that pressure of work caused Donne to resign his duties at Lincoln's Inn. The Benchers showed their appreciation of his services by bestowing on him certain of the privileges of a Bencher. From the time of his appointment to St Paul's Donne was comparatively wealthy, for he continued to hold the living of Sevenoaks. About this time he refused to receive from Sir George More the interest on his wife's dowry, and returned the bond relating to it.

During 1622, apart from his regular duties, Donne was commissioned to preach a sermon explaining the King's recent "Instructions to the Clergy." He also preached before the Honourable Company of the Virginian Plantation. The occasion must have reminded him of the days when he was applying for the secretaryship of the venture. Both sermons were printed.

By 1623 Donne, who had been living upon a reserve of strength accumulated during the travels in Germany, was once again reduced to a very weak state. On October 23 he preached on the occasion of the Serjeants' Feast in the Temple. The sermon was actually delivered at St Paul's, and the whole procession went thither through heavy rain "dabbling on foot and bareheaded." Donne must have caught a severe chill, for he had immediately afterward the most serious illness he had yet suffered. For some time he was expected to die, but gradually recovered. In the course of the illness, which

began with a violent temperature and much
fever, and left him exceedingly weak, he made,
whenever he had sufficient strength to write,
notes on the course of his disease, and recorded extraordinary meditations suggested by
it. These show better than any document he has
left his extraordinary mental activity. Quietude
was absolutely impossible to him, and it seems
safe to conjecture that restlessness of mind
was a major factor in causing his comparatively
early death. During his convalescence he composed the following "hymne."

A HYMNE TO GOD THE FATHER

I

Wilt thou forgive that sinne where I begunne,
  Which was my sin, though it were done
    before ?
Wilt thou forgive that sinne ; through which I
    runne,
  And do run still : though still I do deplore?
    When thou hast done, thou hast not done,
      For I have more.

II

Wilt thou forgive that sinne which I have wonne
  Others to sinne? and, made my sinne their
    doore?
Wilt thou forgive that sinne which I did shunne
  A yeare, or two : but wallowed in, a score?
    When thou hast done, thou hast not done,
      For I have more.

III

I have a sinne of feare, that when I have spunne
  My last thred, I shall perish on the shore;
But sweare by thy selfe, that at my death thy
      sonne
  Shall shine as he shines now, and heretofore;
    And, having done that, Thou haste done,
      I feare no more.

The poem shows that the severe illness turned him back to the contemplation of spiritual matters, and makes it clear that his faith is not yet assured. He recovered to a great extent from this attack, but henceforth he is done with worldly things. His mind seems to move almost exclusively between genuine repentance for sin, horror of death, and a rapt contemplation of God, in which the desire of settled assurance is at times agonizingly apparent.

In 1624 Donne became Vicar of St Dunstan's, of which living he had for long held the reversion. He frequently preached there himself, and it was here that Walton first met the Dean, and became one of his friends.

When in 1625 Charles I came to the throne Donne had to preach before him the first sermon he had heard since his accession, and the Dean awaited the verdict with no little anxiety. The result was reassuring, for he received a command to publish the sermon under the title of "The First Sermon preached before King Charles I." Two months later London was being devastated by the plague, and Donne retired during several

155

months to Chelsea, then a village quite cut off from London. There he stayed at the house of Sir John Danvers, who had lately married Donne's old friend, Mrs Magdalen Herbert. These months were probably the happiest period of the Dean's later years. His letters have no mention of any attack of illness; he was in comfortable surroundings and in daily contact with a lady who was one of the best influences of the latter part of his life. Also resident at Chelsea was George Herbert the poet, seriously considering whether he should take orders. He and Donne were close friends, and there is little doubt that the persuasion of the famous divine had considerable influence on his decision. It is curious to think how different, a few years previously, might have been Donne's advice, but now his heart was fully set upon his spiritual vocation; he had become the visionary orator of Walton's remembrance, the divine whose eloquence harrowed the emotions of his audience.

During this time, when it was not permitted even to call on neighbours, he occupied himself with preparing for the press sermons old and new to the number of eighty, and it was probably during this visit that he composed for his hostess the famous "Autumnall," of which these lines are a part:

No *Spring*, nor *Summer* Beauty hath such grace,
   As I have seen in one *Autumnall* face.
Yong *Beauties* force our love, and that's a *Rape*,
   This doth but *counsaile*, yet you cannot·scape.

If t'were a *shame* to love, here t'were no *shame*
  Affection here takes *Reverences* name.
Were her first yeares the *Golden Age*; That's true,
  But now shee's *gold* oft tried, and ever new.
That was her torrid and inflaming time,
  This is her tolerable *Tropique clyme*.
Faire eyes, who askes more heate then comes
    from hence,
  He in a fever wishes pestilence.
Call not these wrinkles, *graves*; If *graves* they
    were,
  They were *Loves graves*; for else he is no
    where.
Yet lies not Love *dead* here, but here doth sit
  Vow'd to this trench, like an *Anachorit*.
And here, till hers, which must be his *death*, come,
  He doth not digge a *Grave*, but build a *Tombe*.

The poem shows how smooth Donne's verse has become, and exhibits at the same time all his old traits—his genius for a phrase, as "Lanke as an unthrifts purse"; his tendency to grotesqueness, when, in describing very old persons, he says,

Whose *mouthes* are holes, rather worne out, then
  made;

and, lastly, his power of producing an occasional exquisite line. Referring to the end of his life, he has a verse which perhaps Tennyson knew:

I shall ebbe out with them, who home-ward goe.

By December the plague had abated, and in January 1626 the Dean preached from the text,

JOHN DONNE & HIS POETRY

" There was not a house where there was not one dead." During this year he attained the full height of his fame as a preacher, and how great that fame was can be realized only by those who have read the letters of the period, and the poems his death called forth. In the course of the twelve months he preached no fewer than twelve sermons on special occasions. As an addition to his ordinary duties these imposed a severe strain. His health gave way more and more, but he clung to his work. His times of preaching were probably the happiest hours of his life, for in a sermon he could fight out his problem to a victorious finish. As he thundered out his denunciation of sin, as he described in stricken accents the horror of death, he faced his foes; when he turned to consider the power of God he gained confidence, and his voice took on a new ring; as he spoke in winning accents of the mercy and love of God his confidence increased, until faith took fire and he finished the peroration in absolute assurance. But when he was back in his lonely house certainty fell away from him, the exaltation of his own eloquence deserted him, and dim phantoms of doubt, unsubstantial, but to his sensitive spirit no less fatal for that, came haunting him. Small wonder that his preaching held breathless his audience, when he was fighting to subdue what he considered his evil, fleshly self to his spiritual ideal. Only by victory could he win a moment's peace, for his nature knew no compromise. In these last years as he faced his congregation they saw no smooth, plausible, learned priest, but rather a stern, sombre, compelling prophet, a physical wreck marvellously sustained by the will that animated it. We have seen how in his early days he tortured even his pleasures with minute analysis; hear how he now finds sin even in his devotions: '' I throw myself down in my chamber, and I call in and invite God and His angels thither; and when they are there, I neglect God and His angels for the noise of a fly, for the rattling of a coach, for the whining of a door; I talk on, in the same posture of prayer; eyes lifted up, knees bowed down, as though I prayed to God; and if God should ask me when I thought last of God in that prayer I cannot tell.''

In 1627, within the space of one week, he lost two good friends, Lady Danvers and the Countess of Bedford; in 1628 Sir Henry Goodyere and Christopher Brooke died. When, as was his habit, after remaining secluded from Monday till Friday at work upon his sermons, he came forth on Saturday to meet his friends, it must have seemed a dismal entertainment. In August of 1628 he developed a fever, which was complicated by an attack of quinsy. He had to give up all work, retiring to the country, and not returning to London until toward the end of December. Then he disappears from our sight until November of the next year. There is little information to be had of these last years, for he

had almost abandoned the habit of correspondence.   He certainly preached at Paul's Cross in
November, 1629, but that is the only trace of
him.   In 1630 he preached his last sermon in
St Paul's on Easter Day, and in August retired
to his daughter's house at Abury Hatch, Barking.
Writing from there he says : " I am come now,
not only to pay a fever every half year as a
rent for my life; but I am called upon before
the day."   And again: " I have never good
temper, nor good pulse, nor good appetite, nor
good sleep."   His illness was probably a com-
bination of recurrent quinsy and malarial fevers.
In December he insisted on returning to London.
His friend Dr Foxe persuaded him to try drinking milk.   This he did for ten days, after which
he told Foxe " that he would not drink it ten
days longer, upon the best moral assurance of
having twenty years added to his life; for he
loved it not."   He was appointed to preach on
the first Friday in Lent, and insisted on under-
taking it, but when he appeared many of the
audience "thought he presented himself not
to preach mortification by a living voice, but
mortality by a decayed body and a dying face."
At first he faltered, but gained strength as he
proceeded.   The effect of such sentences as the
following, which is practically the burden of
this last lament, must in the circumstances have
been appalling.   "That which we call life is
but *Hebdomada mortium*, a week of death,
seven days, seven periods of our life spent in

dying, a dying seven times over, and there is an
end. Our birth dies in infancy, and our infancy
dies in youth, and youth and the rest die in age,
and age also dies and determines all.'' A last
grim facing of the fact! After the sermon
Donne returned to his house to leave it no more
alive. His preparations for passing were made
elaborately. He had himself painted life-size,
wrapped in his winding-sheet with the end turned
back so that his face could be seen, and he kept
the picture with him until he died. The monu-
ment in St Paul's was studied from this painting.

Five weeks after preaching his last sermon—
afterward printed under the grim title of
'' Death's Duel ''—he took to his bed. He had
set his affairs in order, had interviewed and bade
farewell to all his friends. This was about
March 16. As he lay there with the last sands
of his time running out, on March 23 he composed the following poem, his last:

HYMNE TO GOD MY GOD, IN MY SICKNESSE

Since I am comming to that Holy roome,
   Where, with thy Quire of Saints for evermore,
I shall be made thy Musique; As I come
   I tune the Instrument here at the dore,
   And what I must doe then, thinke here before.

Whilst my Physitians by their love are growne
   Cosmographers, and I their Mapp, who lie
Flat on this bed, that by them may be showne
   That this is my South-west discoverie
   Per fretum febris, by these streights to die,

L   161

I joy, that in these straits, I see my West;
  For, though theire currants yeeld returne to
    none,
What shall my West hurt me? As West and
    East
  In all flatt Maps (and I am one) are one,
  So death doth touch the Resurrection.

Is the Pacifique Sea my home? Or are
  The Easterne riches? Is *Ierusalem?*
Anyan, and *Magellan,* and *Gibraltare,*
  All streights, and none but streights, are wayes
    to them,
  Whether where *Iaphet* dwelt, or *Cham,* or *Sem.*

     .   .   .   .

So, in his purple wrapp'd receive mee Lord,
  By these his thornes give me his other Crowne;
And as to others soules I preach'd thy word,
  Be this my Text, my Sermon to mine owne,
  Therfore that he may raise the Lord throws down.

This poem is an amazing tribute to the
vitality of Donne. That eight days before his
death he could write with such vigour, with
such originality, and in a manner so characteristic is little short of marvellous. The piece
has also a subdued note of confidence that one
is glad to catch.

He lay thus fifteen days and died on March 31,
1631. Walton was confident that at the last
he had a vision, "and being satisfied with this
blessed sight, as his soul ascended, and his last
breath departed from him, he closed his own
eyes, and then disposed his hands and body into

such a posture, as required not the least alteration by those that came to shroud him.

"Thus variable, thus virtuous was the life; thus excellent, thus exemplary was the death of this memorable man."

For Walton it was Donne the divine alone that counted; we have been preoccupied with Donne the poet, the man whose leaping imagination we have seen at work, though too frequently it is hidden from us by the dazzle of a subtle intellect. Considering his love of precision and his fondness for realistic imagery one is inclined to suspect in Donne a brilliant scientist who forced his genius through the mould of verse, and applied a scientific bent of mind to a study of intangible emotions. This would account for his frequently unpoetical figures and his excessive ingenuity—he was working in the wrong medium. His great successes are at moments when emotion has raised his mind out of the plane of fancy into that of imagination. Yet his vast contemporary influence was based on his ingenuity. His many imitators, from George Herbert to Abraham Cowley and Dryden in his early years, with one accord emulate not the direct forcefulness of his best manner, but the singularities of his expression. It is only in Restoration times that we see the satire and the poetry of reason which he initiated bearing fruit in Dryden's virile couplets.

Yet not the divine and the poet combined will

give us more than a partial conception of the man. To obtain a proper estimate of Donne it is imperative that his universality should be appreciated. He was the greatest pulpit orator of his day. All England was at his feet on account of his eloquence. He was one of the most learned theologians of the time. His skill in affairs was such that he was fitter to serve a king than a subject. He was noted for his knowledge of the law, which at one time he thought of practising. He mastered the medical science of his time. His correct interpretation of the effects of the dark beginnings of our modern science places him on a level with Mr H. G. Wells for piercing insight. In subtle juggling with ideas and images he would have beaten Mr Chesterton on his own ground. He was, moreover, a real though unequal poet—occasionally a great one. Such an assemblage of powers makes him gigantic. And during the last decade of his life we see this man striving through prayer and fasting, supplication and starvation, to achieve a perfect faith in the God of his fathers, with Whom he longed for a close communion. The lion in the path was his magnificent intellect, the finest perhaps of his generation, which would not consent to be permanently subdued. Doubtless at times Donne reached the desired stage of realization, but his poetry and sermons both show that his victory was never assured. The struggle had ever and again to be renewed, until the worn-out body

164

collapsed under the strain. The attempt to harmonize the conflicting elements of his character could not be wholly successful; his mind was too powerful to be subdued to the pattern of faith which he had inherited; yet what a man might do, he did. Never did he relinquish his struggle to attain that truth of which he said:

On a huge hill,
Cragged, and steep, Truth stands, and hee that will
Reach her, about must, and about must goe;
And what the hills suddennes resists, winne so.

BIBLIOGRAPHY

The following volumes may be specially recommended for use in a further study of Donne and his work.

TEXT

"The Poems of John Donne." Edited by Professor H. J. C. Grierson. 2 vols. Oxford University Press.

"Poetical Works of John Donne." Edited by Sir E. K. Chambers, with an introduction by Professor George Saintsbury. 2 vols. Routledge.

BIOGRAPHY AND CRITICISM

"The Life and Letters of Dr John Donne." By Sir Edmund Gosse. 2 vols. Heinemann.

"John Donne : a Study in Discord." By Hugh I'Anson Fausset. Cape.

"A Study of the Prose Works of John Donne." By Evelyn M. Simpson. Oxford University Press.

D

CPSIA information can be obtained
at www.ICGtesting.com
Printed in the USA
BVHW031811230622
640527BV00007B/84